MENTAL FILES
IN FLUX

FRANÇOIS RECANATI

Great Clarendon Street, Oxford, OX2 6DP,
United Kingdom

Oxford University Press is a department of the University of Oxford.
It furthers the University's objective of excellence in research, scholarship,
and education by publishing worldwide. Oxford is a registered trade mark of
Oxford University Press in the UK and in certain other countries

Published in the United States of America by Oxford University Press
198 Madison Avenue, New York, NY 10016, United States of America

British Library Cataloguing in Publication Data

Data available

Library of Congress Cataloging in Publication Data

Data available

ISBN 978–0–19–879035–8 (Hbk.)
ISBN 978–0–19–879036–5 (Pbk.)

MENTAL FILES IN FLUX

Mental Files in Flux is a sequel to François Recanati's *Mental Files* (OUP, 2012). The author pursues the exploration of the mental file framework for thinking about concepts and singular reference.

Mental files are based on 'epistemically rewarding' relations to objects in the environment. Standing in such relations to objects puts the subject in a position to gain information regarding them. The information thus gained goes into the file based on the relevant relation. Files do not merely store information about objects, however, they refer to them and serve as singular terms in the language of thought, with a relational (nondescriptivist) semantics. In this framework, the reference of linguistic expressions is inherited from that of the files we associate with them. Crucially, files also play the role of 'modes of presentation'. They are used to account for cognitive significance phenomena illustrated by so-called 'Frege cases'.

In this new volume, Recanati considers what happens to mental files in a dynamic setting. Mental files are construed as both continuants (dynamic files) and as time-slices thereof (static files). Dynamic files are needed to account for confusion, recognition and tracking. *Mental Files in Flux* considers what happens to the relation of coreference *de jure*, central to the functional characterization of files, when one adopts a dynamic perspective. Only a weak form of coreference *de jure* is said to hold between stages of the same dynamic file. The second part of the book argues that communication involves *interpersonal* dynamic files. Special attention is paid to the communication of indexical thoughts (de se contents) and communication using proper names.

LINES OF THOUGHT
This series is published in association with the Aristotelian Society

François Recanati is a philosopher of language and mind based in Paris. His published works include *Meaning and Force* (CUP 1988), *Direct Reference: From Language to Thought* (Blackwell 1993), *Oratio Obliqua, Oratio Recta* (MIT Press/Bradford Books 2000), *Literal Meaning* (CUP 2004), *Perspectival Thought* (OUP 2007), *Truth-Conditional Pragmatics* (OUP 2010) and *Mental Files* (OUP 2012). He is a Foreign Honorary Member of the American Academy of Arts and Sciences, an honorary doctor of Stockholm University, a recipient of the CNRS silver medal, and a Professor at College de France.

Lines of Thought

Short philosophical books

Published in association with the Aristotelian Society

Series editor: Scott Sturgeon

Hume Variations
Jerry A. Fodor

Moral Fictionalism
Mark Eli Kalderon

Perfectionism and the Common Good: Themes in the Philosophy of T. H. Green
David O. Brink

Knowledge and Practical Interests
Jason Stanley

Thought and Reality
Michael Dummett

Our Knowledge of the Internal World
Robert C. Stalnaker

Mental Files in Flux
François Recanati

Understanding 'I': Language and Thought
José Luis Bermúdez

Contents

Preface

MENTAL files are cognitive structures which store information about entities. They are entries in the mental encyclopedia, that is, concepts. Some, following Grice (1969), construe them as *collections* of information units, but I prefer to think of them as akin to *containers* ('concrete cognitive particulars', as Crimmins and Perry 1989 say). The identity of a collection is determined by the identity of its elements, but the identity of a container is independent of that of its contents.

Concepts are the constituents of thought, so the question arises, what is it for a mental file to be deployed in (occurrent) thought? I take it that a file is deployed in thought only if it has a sufficient degree of activation (whatever that amounts to in neural terms). An active file gives access to the information it contains, and contributes its reference to the semantic content of the thought. However, a mental file only contributes its reference to the semantic content of *the thought of which it is a constituent*. To be a constituent of a given thought it is not sufficient to be active when the other constituents are. As Fodor and Pylyshyn point out, 'when representations express concepts that belong to the same [thought], they are not merely simultaneously active, but also *in construction with each other*' (Fodor and Pylyshyn 1988: 25). I will not have anything special to say about the constituency issue here—I merely assume that constituency is somehow encoded in the brain.

In this book, as in my previous book *Mental Files*, I am mainly concerned with singular concepts (mental files about individuals). The semantic contribution of a (singular) file to the content of the thought in which it occurs is the individual it refers to—itself a constituent of the singular proposition which is the content of the thought.

The *reference* of a file is determined relationally, not satisfaction-ally (Bach 1987). It is *not* whatever fits the body of information in the file. The relations which determine the reference of a file are *ER relations* (epistemically rewarding relations) in which the subject who deploys the file stands to entities in the environment. ER relations make information flow possible, and the information which reaches the subject thanks to a given ER relation goes into the file based on that relation. (To say that a file is 'based on' some ER relation is to say that it is deployed only if the ER relation is presumed to hold.)

What about the units of information contained in a file? On my view, files only contain *predicative* elements. The fact that a predicate-like information unit is stored in a given file is what secures the 'subject' bit—what the predicate is predicated of (namely the reference of the file). Because it is determined on relational grounds, the reference of the file is, to a very large extent, independent of the information it contains.

The ER relations on which indexical files/concepts (HERE, NOW, THIS) are based are relevant to perception and action (Perry 1993). They are acquaintance relations in the narrow sense. Encyclopedia entries are more objective files, detached from specific ER relations, but even they are based on an evolving network of ER relations through which the reference of the file is determined. Some of these relations to the reference are mediated by the linguistic community, as in the historical chain picture of communication. They are acquaintance relations only in an extended sense.

Although they are mental representations rather than semantic objects, mental files play many of the roles which Frege assigned to 'senses'.[1] Like senses, files are transparent: the subject knows when

---

[1] There are three main differences with Frege. First, files are mental particulars, not abstract objects. Second, Fregean senses determine reference absolutely, while files determine reference only with respect to the context of deployment (at a particular time). Third, in contrast to Fregean senses, files are not associated with expressions as a matter of linguistic encoding. File deployment is an aspect of the

she is deploying the same file twice, and when she is deploying distinct files.[2] Like senses, files come to be associated with linguistic expressions and determine their reference: in my framework, the reference of an expression is the reference of the file associated with it.[3] Finally, like senses, files play the role of modes of presentation. Frege's Constraint states that if a rational subject can believe of a given object both that it is F and that it is not F (as happens in so-called 'Frege cases'), then the subject thinks of that object under distinct modes of presentation (Schiffer 1978: 180). Mental files are particularly suited to play the mode of presentation role. The subject's having distinct mental files about a given object is arguably sufficient to generate the possibility of Frege cases, even if the files contain the same information about the referent.[4]

In addition to playing the classical Fregean roles, mental files also play a key role in what Kit Fine (2007) calls 'semantic coordination'. If two token singular terms M and N are associated with the *same* file, it is presupposed that they corefer (if they refer at all) and

psychological process of interpreting an utterance, a process that is highly sensitive to context. A given expression will typically be associated with different files in different contexts (even for the same subject). What is *conventionally* associated with a referring expression (as part of its linguistic meaning) is not a file, but a constraint on files, which has the effect of coordinating the files deployed by the speech protagonists.

[2] A reader for Oxford University Press objected to the transparency claim on the grounds that ordinary subjects cannot be credited with theoretically sophisticated higher order beliefs about the mental files they deploy. My account of coreference *de jure* in terms of knowledge of the coreference relation raises the same kind of objection (as another OUP reviewer pointed out): ordinary subjects cannot be credited with theoretically sophisticated beliefs about coreference relations holding between the terms they use. But when I claim that ordinary subjects know certain things, I take this 'knowledge' to be manifested through the subjects' dispositions and behaviour, without requiring on their part the ability to make the knowledge in question explicit.

[3] That means that Strawson and ordinary language philosophers were right: referring is not something an expression does—it's something language users do when they use an expression (Strawson 1971: 8). See Recanati (2018) for the connection between contextualism in the philosophy of language and the mental file approach to singular reference.

[4] This is actually debatable. See Gray (2016) for discussion.

'trading upon identity' becomes valid: one can move from 'M is *F*' and 'N is *G*' directly to 'there is an *x* which is *F* and *G*', without needing to invoke an identity premiss (Campbell 1987). In such a case M and N are said to be semantically coordinated, or coreferential *de jure*. Coreference *de jure*—a topic that looms large in this book—is not just a feature of language or discourse: it is an essential feature of our cognition. There is coreference *de jure* in thought whenever the subject goes through what Millikan (1997, 2000) refers to as a 'mediate inference' relying on a presupposition of identity.

* * *

I have just summarized the main tenets of the mental file framework. In this book I deal with a set of potentially problematic issues that have been thought to threaten its viability, or the viability of any attempt to resurrect the Fregean approach.

First, there is an apparent tension between the transparency thesis and externalism about content. If the reference of a file depends upon the world (which object stands at the other end of the ER relation) then knowing that the same file is deployed twice does not guarantee that, on these distinct occurrences, the file refers to the same thing. Equivocation is always possible. As Millikan puts it:

What is the guarantee [. . .] that the referents of duplicate thoughts actually *are* the same? Or if what you mean by 'duplicate thoughts' *includes* that they have the same referent, what is to guarantee that the mind that grasps two thoughts can tell whether these thoughts are indeed duplicates? How can there be uninformative identities that are at the same time certain really to be identities and not merely false appearances of identity? This line of questioning highlights the internalist assumption built into the Fregean position. What is duplicated when 'the very same thought' is repeated has to be something which is at the same time (1) compelled always to bring with it the same referent and (2) capable of being unmistakably known by the mind (while the mind is doubly entertaining it) as being the very same thought.   (Millikan 1997: 516)

In other words, there is a tension between two alleged features of Fregean senses and whatever plays the mode of presentation role: they can't be simultaneously transparent to the mind and determine reference. Or at least, the tension arises as soon as one gives up 'the internalist assumption built up into the Fregean position'.

Millikan's critique of Fregean internalism casts doubt on the very notion of coreference *de jure*. In the Fregean framework I espouse, coreference *de jure* is coreference that is known a priori, because it holds in virtue of meaning and meaning is transparent. According to Millikan, there is no such thing. Externalism precludes transparency. There is tracking and tracking presupposes identity of reference, but tracking is always fallible: the subject keeps track of an object dynamically, and may occasionally lose track, even she does not realize she has lost track.[5]

Another tension, internal to my framework, has been identified in several reviews of *Mental Files*.[6] As I describe them, mental files play two potentially conflicting roles: the mode of presentation role (to account for Frege cases in accordance with Frege's Constraint) and the semantic coordination role (to enable coreference *de jure*). There is a potential conflict because coreference *de jure* can hold *across* ER relations but, *qua* modes of presentation, files are typed *by* ER relations and are only deployed when the relevant ER relation is assumed to hold. Because of that problem, Papineau (2013) suggests giving up the indexical files and their associated ER relations, and doing everything with encyclopedia entries

---

[5] 'There is never an a priori guarantee that one has kept track. The same is true of recognitional abilities. You may know, for example, literally hundreds of ways to identify each member of your immediate family, some of which ways—a long look full into your spouse's face in full daylight, for example—may (barring removal of your brain to a vat) actually be infallible. But if that is so, it is because the world, not anything in your mind, is constructed so as to make it so. It is because there is not in fact any other person in the world who looks just like that in the face (and no one actually able, and desirous of, putting your brain in a vat)—a convenient fact but not one guaranteed by a priori reflection' (Millikan 1997: 517).

[6] See Papineau 2013, Onofri 2015, Ball 2015, and Ninan 2015. See also Prosser forthcoming.

('detached files', as Perry calls them). Evans had already suggested moving to a 'dynamic' notion of mode of presentation that persists through changes of ER relations (Evans 1981). Pressure in the same direction comes from another problem: the problem of communication. If the thoughts entertained by the speaker involve files based on specific ER relations, how can the speaker communicate these indexical thoughts to an addressee who does not stand in the same ER relations to the reference?

The tension between the two roles is apparent in the following example, due to Ruth Millikan:

Consider the dynamic mode of presentation involved as you perceptually track a person, Kate, to whom you have just been introduced at a party. For a brief moment—not much longer, suppose, than a saccade—you divert your eyes to the face of a friend, but immediately pick up Kate's face again. Then a large fat man, excusing himself, passes between you and Kate, but again you immediately pick up the track. Looking at Kate and hearing her voice, you perceive these as having the same source, as locating the same person. Now Kate passes for a moment into another room, but you continue to hear her voice—though of course there are spaces between the words and she soon emerges again. By now she is beginning both to look and to sound quite familiar, so that after stepping outside for a moment, you immediately find her again. The time interval was longer this time than between her words, but short enough for her voice still to be 'in your ears'.   (Millikan 1997: 511–12)

The fact that many distinct ER relations succeed each other does not prevent tracking and trading on identity (coreference *de jure*). That is the justification for Evans's postulation of 'dynamic Fregean senses': modes of presentation as continuants spanning a diversity of ER relations. But dynamic modes of presentation are coarse-grained, and we need finer-grained modes of presentation based on specific ER relations to deal with Frege cases. At any point in the sequence, the subject can wonder whether or not the tracked individual is the same; that is only possible if the various ER relations (hearing the voice, seeing the face, etc.) determine distinct modes of presentation. Because of this tension, Millikan says, we lack

a clear principle of individuation—of sameness and difference—[...] for [modes of presentation]. When did you leave off one 'ability to track' and start using another 'ability to track', or some different kind of ability to 'know which object you are thinking about', as you collected information over time about Kate?   (Millikan 1997: 512)

Millikan concludes on a sceptical note:

The notion of modes of presentation is not a useful notion for any theorist who has befriended mental representations, nor for any who has befriended externalism about thought content. The reason is that there is no principled way to individuate modes of presentation on these views, or to achieve any of the various effects for the sake of which Frege introduced them. (Millikan 1997: 518)

★ ★ ★

In this book I do my best to ease the tensions, and to solve the problems, without giving up any of the main tenets of the mental file framework. I keep the fine-grained ER relations, used to account for indexical thought and Frege cases. But, in the spirit of Evans and Papineau, I introduce dynamic files, which are sequences of files in the static sense. Relatedly, I show that there are two distinct notions of coreference *de jure*, corresponding to distinct phenomena. Both notions are compatible with the lack of actual coreference,[7] so Millikan's externalist objection to transparency does not apply. (Transparency no longer entails the impossibility of equivocation.)

---

[7] That means that there can be coreference *de jure* (of either sort) without actual coreference. Because that is so, the phrase 'coreference *de jure*' is somewhat misleading (since it suggests that coreference *de jure* is a kind of coreference).

At the dynamic level, as in tracking or recognition, only weak coreference *de jure* holds. Weak coreference *de jure* is not a transitive relation. But strong coreference *de jure*—the relation that holds between *synchronous* deployments of the same file—is transitive and can ground identity for mental files. The tension which gives rise to Millikan's individuation problem is relaxed by distinguishing two types of file: static files (or file-stages), which account for cognitive significance and Frege cases, and dynamic files, which underlie tracking, recognition, and information update. Dynamic files are construed as continuants (temporal sequences of stages), susceptible to growth, fusion, and fission; static files are time-slices thereof. As for the communication problem, dealt with in the second part of the book, it is solved by giving up the naïve view that sees communication as (necessarily) the replication of thought. Like information update, communication is shown to bring dynamic files into motion (interpersonal dynamic files, in the case of communication).

* * *

I said that static files (or file-stages) account for cognitive significance and Frege cases:

At any point in the [dynamic] sequence, the subject can wonder whether or not the tracked individual is the same; that is only possible if the various ER relations (hearing the voice, seeing the face, etc.) determine distinct modes of presentation.

In this framework the *possibility of Frege cases* provides the basis for individuating modes of presentation construed as static files. Two modes of presentation are said to be distinct whenever it is rationally *possible* for the subject to wonder whether, through their deployment, he or she is thinking about the same thing. It is that Fregean criterion which forces us to posit (static) modes of presentation as fine-grained as the ER relations they are based on, in addition to the 'dynamic modes of presentation' which span successive ER relations to the reference. But the criterion cannot be merely taken for granted. It is in need of clarification and justification.

The Fregean criterion of difference can be formulated in two different ways. One formulation is modal, the other not. The modal version is what I have just invoked to ground fine-grained files based on specific ER relations:

> Two modes of presentation m and m' are distinct if it is *possible* for the subject to entertain doubts as to whether, through their deployment, he or she is thinking about the same thing.

The non-modal version does not talk about what is possible, but about what is actual:

> Two modes of presentation m and m' are distinct if the subject entertains doubts as to whether, through their deployment, he or she is thinking about the same thing.

The non-modal version is fine as far as it goes, Papineau says, but the modal version is objectionable. Since the modal version is that which the fine-grained mental file theorist appeals to, so much the worse for that theory.[8]

The modal version is susceptible to criticism on the grounds that it multiplies mental files beyond necessity. It is *always* possible for a rational subject to doubt whether, e.g., the object he sees is the object he touches, *even if the subject actually harbours no doubt at all.* But if the subject harbours no doubt at all and merely presupposes the identity of the seen object and the touched object, *then* he or she thinks of the object under a single, multi-modal mode of presentation, rather than under two distinct modes of presentation (visual and haptic). This shows that the sheer *possibility* of Frege cases is not sufficient to establish the distinctness of modes of presentation, hence the distinctness of files. Only *actual Frege*

---

[8] That argument was made by Papineau in conversation during the Istanbul workshop on Mental Files mentioned in note 11.

cases count in this respect. The Fregean criterion as used by the fine-grained theorist—i.e. the modal version of the criterion—must be rejected, because of its illegitimate appeal to *potential* Frege cases. So the Papineau argument goes.

The argument fails (I believe) because the fine-grained theorist appeals to *both* potential and actual Frege cases. They have different roles to play in the theory, in connection with the type/token distinction for modes of presentation.

Potential Frege cases are used to individuate modes of presentation construed as types. Two mode of presentation types m and m' are distinct just in case it is *possible* for a rational subject to entertain doubts as to whether, through their deployment, he or she is thinking about the same thing. But when it comes to token modes of presentation, what counts is *doubt actually harboured*, not doubt that is merely possible. In a situation in which a subject trades upon the identity of the object seen and the object touched, what is deployed is a *single* mental file, based on several ER relations. The file is of a distinctive type, based on a composite ER relation. Identity of the object seen and the object touched is presupposed through the compounding of ER relations. That is, obviously, compatible with the possibility for the subject to *come to doubt* that the object seen is the object touched, i.e. to *stop* presupposing the identity. Coming to doubt is a dynamic operation which amounts to 'splitting' the composite file. This can always happen, but the sheer *possibility* of doubt is not sufficient to entail that two distinct files are *actually* deployed (before the split). The tokens that are deployed are individuated by the subject's *actual* dispositions at the time of deployment.[9]

✦ ✦ ✦

[9] In the following passage, Heck seems to have difficulties sorting out the roles played by actual Frege cases and potential Frege cases in establishing the distinctness of modes of presentation. 'A few weeks ago', he says, 'I was looking outside the window of my study when I saw a cat who looked very much like my cat, Joe. Joe is an indoor cat. But, as I realized after a minute or two, that cat *was* Joe, who had apparently escaped to the great outdoors. In so recognizing Joe, I was making an

I am indebted to all of those who have discussed my views, both in print and in conversation. They are my direct interlocutors in this book. I have learnt much from those who contributed to the various recent books or journal issues devoted to mental files,[10] or participated in the meetings that were organized around my work.[11] I also benefitted greatly from the comments and suggestions made by the participants in my 2015 EHESS seminar on

identity judgment: *That* creature—the one presented to me visually, in such and such a way—is Joe. One can see that two "modes of presentation" must be involved here by reflecting on the fact that I did not originally recognize Joe, and *the structure of the phenomenon would not have been different had I recognized him immediately. Even if I had, I could intelligibly have wondered whether that creature really was Joe'* (Heck 2012: 138–9, emphasis mine). I agree with Heck that two distinct token modes of presentation were deployed before recognition occurred, but I deny that 'the structure of the phenomenon would not have been different had [Heck] recognized [Joe] immediately'. Had Heck recognized Joe immediately, there would have been a single token mode of presentation at stake, rather than two distinct token modes of presentation. The last sentence is supposed to provide an argument for there being two modes of presentation even in a case of immediate recognition, but this argument is based on the unactualized *possibility* of doubt. I agree with Papineau that no such argument can establish that two distinct token modes of presentation are deployed in 'immediate recognition' cases.

[10] Two special issues, of *Disputatio* (in 2013) and of *Inquiry* (in 2015), have been dedicated to my 2012 book; I am grateful to Fiora Salis and Herman Cappelen for setting them up. Two other volumes on the topic of mental files have just been published or are currently in press: a special issue of the *Review of Philosophy and Psychology* (*Mental Files*, edited by M. Murez and myself, 2016), and *Singular Thought and Mental Files* (edited by R. Goodman, J. Genone, and N. Kroll for Oxford University Press).

[11] There were three such workshops in 2014—at Université Paris-Sorbonne in March (organized by Pascal Ludwig and Jean-Baptiste Rauzy), at Università di Modena e Reggio Emilia in May (organized by Annalisa Coliva and Michele Palmira), and at the University of St Andrews in October (organized by Herman Cappelen)—as well as, in April, an 'Author-meets-critics' session on *Mental Files* at the Pacific APA, San Diego (set up by Krista Lawlor) and a day-long meeting with students on the same topic at the University of Toronto (set up by Imogen Dickie). I am much indebted to the organizers of these events and to all of those who participated. I am also indebted to Eleanora Orlando and Justina Diaz Legaspe (as well as Ramiro Caso, Nicolás LoGuercio, Alfonso Losada, Laura Skerk, and Ezequiel Zerbudis) for the Buenos Aires workshop on mental files and singular reference they organized in October 2013, and to Lucas Thorpe and Andrea Onofri for setting up another workshop ('Thinking of the Same—A Workshop on Mental Files') in Istanbul in September 2015.

mental files, where I presented the first part of the book, and from those made by the editors of and reviewers for various OUP volumes including papers of mine overlapping in content with this book.[12] Finally, I am grateful to Robert May, Ángel Pinillos, and two readers for Oxford University Press for useful comments which helped me prepare the final version.

[12] See my papers 'Coreference *de jure*', in R. Goodman et al. (eds), *Singular Thought and Mental Files* (Recanati forthcoming); 'Cognitive Dynamics', in M. de Ponte and K. Korta (eds), *Reference and Representation in Thought and Language* (Recanati 2017); and 'Indexical Thought: The Communication Problem', in M. Garcia-Carpintero and S. Torre (eds), *About Oneself* (Recanati 2016).

Part I

Coreference *De Jure* and the Flow of Information

I

Coreference De Jure in the Mental File Framework

1.1. *The Phenomenon*

Two singular terms are coreferential whenever they refer to the same object. Coreference is *de facto* when the two terms merely *happen* to refer to the same object. Sometimes, however, coreference seems to be predetermined, and arguably guaranteed, in an a priori manner. This stronger form of coreference has been given several names in the literature, e.g. 'presupposed coreference' (Fauconnier 1974: 7–8, Büring 2005: 154), 'stipulated coreference' (Kamp and Reyle 1993: 257–60), 'grammatically determined coreference' (Fiengo and May 1996: 122, 2006: 37), 'explicit coreference' (Taylor 2003), 'strict coreference' (Fine 2007), 'internal coreference' (Lawlor 2010), and 'coreference *de jure*' (Neale 2005, Pinillos 2011, Recanati 2012, Goodsell 2014).[1] The phenomenon is well known, but there is disagreement regarding its proper analysis.

---

[1] Other appellations include 'intended coreference' (Kamp 1990: 48), 'presumed coreference' (Lawlor 2001), 'coco-reference' (Perry 2012b: 172), and 'assumed coreference' (Gibbard 2012: 269–70), among others. It is not obvious that there is a single phenomenon at stake, however (see Section 2.1; see also Goodsell 2014 on the distinction between coreference *de jure* and 'assumed coreference').

Fine provides the following criterion for (what I will continue to call) coreference *de jure*:

A good test of when an object is represented as the same[2] is in terms of whether one might sensibly raise the question of whether it is the same. An object is represented as the same in a piece of discourse only if *no one who understands the discourse can sensibly raise the question of whether it is the same*.   (Fine 2007: 40, emphasis mine)

The paradigm case is anaphora. A pronoun and its referential antecedent are coreferential *de jure*: there is no way in which the anaphoric pronoun might not refer to the same thing as the antecedent (assuming the antecedent itself refers). This is guaranteed linguistically, so Fine's criterion applies: whoever has fully understood the statement cannot doubt that there is coreference between the pronoun and its referential antecedent.[3] Coreference, in such cases, is a matter of meaning.

But anaphora is only a special case. There is coreference *de jure* also between two occurrences of the same name-type. As Fine puts it,

Suppose that you say 'Cicero is an orator' and later say 'Cicero was honest,' intending to make the very same use of the name 'Cicero.' Then anyone who raises the question of whether the reference was the same would thereby betray his lack of understanding of what you meant. (Fine 2007: 40)

Taylor claims that proper names are *essentially* devices of coreference. Their role is to build, and exploit, 'chains of explicit coreference',

---

[2] When two singular terms are coreferential *de jure*, Fine says that they '*represent (their referent) as the same*'. In contrast, an explicit identity statement such as 'Cicero is Tully' is said to represent the referent of the two singular terms as *being* the same. The two names are not coreferential *de jure* in the identity statement (see note 3), so they do not 'represent their referent as the same'.

[3] In the case of identity statements such as 'Cicero is Tully', one *can* doubt that there is coreference between the two names, hence doubt the *truth* of the statement, even though one fully understands it.

participation in which guarantees the sharing of subject matter with other participants. 'What it is to intend to use an expression as a name', he says, 'is to use that expression with the intention of either launching or continuing a chain of explicit coreference' (Taylor 2003: 10). When the same name is used twice, coreference is linguistically guaranteed: 'Tokens of the same name are guaranteed to corefer, if they refer at all' (Taylor 2003: 14–15).[4] The fact that different objects may bear (what sounds superficially like) the same name is, from this point of view, an accident, irrelevant to the design of language. Such homonymous names have to be treated as distinct names for the purposes of logico-linguistic analysis (Kripke 1980) or, better perhaps, as distinct *expressions* (i.e. syntactic types) made up of the same name (Fiengo and May 1998, 2006).[5] 'Names are vocabulary items', Fiengo and May write, 'and expressions are syntactic items that may contain names . . . A name, qua lexical item, may in principle occur in *m*-many syntactic expression-types, each of which may have *n*-many token occurrences' (Fiengo and May 2006: 14–17). When the speaker who makes two successive utterances of 'Cicero' 'intend[s] to make the very same use of the name "Cicero"' (as Fine puts it), he produces two occurrences of the same expression; but a homonymous name (say 'Cicero' as the name of a cat) would be a different expression, made up of the same name.

In addition to the test suggested by Fine, there is another way of testing for coreference *de jure*. Two terms α and β are coreferential *de jure* just in case they licence a pattern of inference which John Campbell (1987) famously dubbed 'Trading on Identity' (TI):

---

[4] In addition to the norm that *distinct occurrences of the same name corefer*, Taylor puts forward a second norm governing proper names: *occurrences of distinct name types refer to distinct objects*. The second norm will not play any role in my discussion.

[5] Fiengo and May generalize to all 'expressions' what Taylor says about names: 'All tokens of a given expression [. . .] corefer, *as a matter of grammar*' (Fiengo and May 2006: 18). Coreference *de jure*, for them, is a matter of type identity in all cases. As we shall see (Section 1.2), this view leads them to treat an anaphoric pronoun and its antecedent as two distinct realizations of the same expression (the same syntactic type).

Trading on Identity (TI)

α is F

β is G

Therefore, something is both F and G.

Trading on Identity is licensed when the same name occurs in both premisses, as in (1) below, or when the singular term in the second premiss is anaphoric on the singular term in the first premiss, as in (2):

(1)　Cicero is F

　　　Cicero is G

　　　Therefore, someone is both F and G

(2)　Cicero_i is F

　　　he_i is G

　　　Therefore, someone is both F and G.

In the absence of either recurrence or anaphora, however, TI is not licensed: an additional identity premiss is needed to reach the conclusion, as illustrated by (3):

(3)　Cicero is F

　　　Tully is G

　　　Cicero = Tully

　　　Therefore, someone is both F and G.

1.2. *Recurrence*

Fiengo and May claim that coreference *de jure* is a matter of recurrence (type identity) in *all* cases, and not merely in the cases in which the same proper name occurs twice. In general,

> Occurrences of an expression type corefer if they refer at all; all occurrences in a given discourse will be coindexed, and hence coreferential as a matter of representation.　(Fiengo and May 1998: 381)

When the same expression recurs, it carries the same semantic value; that's the general principle. This explains why two occurrences of the same name (qua syntactic expression) corefer *de jure*. But Fiengo and May take the recurrence account to apply to anaphora as well. They treat an anaphoric expression and its antecedent as *two distinct realizations of the same expression* (the same abstract 'syntactic' type), despite the lack of morphophonemic identity between them (Fiengo and May 1996: 137). In their framework, just as two distinct 'syntactic expressions' may involve the same lexical item (say, the same homonymous name), what counts as the same expression from the *syntactic* point of view may sometimes involve distinct items (a name and a pronoun).[6] Both types of case are illustrated by sentence (4):

> (4) After their first meeting, Aristotle$_1$ invited Jackie$_2$ to spend a week on his$_1$ yacht. She$_2$ was then readings the *Metaphysics*, where Aristotle$_3$ says that knowledge is a basic human need.

In this sentence the numerical indices track type identity at the underlying syntactic level. The two occurrences of 'Aristotle' in (4) are tokens of distinct expressions (one, *Aristotle$_1$*, referring to the shipping magnate Aristotle Onassis, the other, *Aristotle$_3$*, referring to the ancient philosopher), while the anaphoric pronoun 'she' in the second sentence counts as the same expression as its antecedent in the first sentence, in virtue of being syntactically coindexed. As a result, Trading on Identity is licensed in the latter case (*Jackie$_2$/she$_2$*) but not in the former (*Aristotle$_1$/Aristotle$_3$*). (4) allows the inference to (5):

> (5) Onassis invited someone who was then reading the *Metaphysics*.

---

[6] 'Two NPs may be occurrences of the same syntactic expression even though one may contain the name 'John' and the other the pronoun 'he'; binding theory proceeds on this assumption' (Fiengo and May 1998: 383).

But the inference from (4) to (6) is not licensed, because the two occurrences of the name 'Aristotle' bear different indices and do not count as tokens of the same expression:

(6)   Someone for whom knowledge is a basic need invited Jackie on his yacht.

The idea that an anaphoric expression is the same expression as its antecedent is reminiscent of an early stage of transformational grammar, when an anaphoric pronoun was taken to be a transformation of a copy of its antecedent. 'Martin sold his car' was analysed as derived from 'Martin sold Martin's car' by a pronoun transformation, a condition of which is the syntactic identity between the pronominalized term and its antecedent. Because different individuals may be called 'Martin', the syntactic identity was taken to include the identity of the referential index: in 'Martin$_1$ sold Martin$_1$'s car', there is syntactic identity, but in 'Martin$_1$ sold Martin$_2$'s car' there isn't, so pronominalization (leading to 'Martin sold his car') is only possible in the former case. Generative linguistics has given up the idea that pronouns result from a transformation of (a copy of) their antecedent, but Fiengo and May retain the idea of a syntactic identity, corresponding to coindexing, between the pronoun and its antecedent.

Fiengo and May's use of 'expression' is somewhat counter-intuitive because (in the case of anaphora) it abstracts from issues of morphophonemic identity. Moreover, special problems may be thought to arise in connection with examples involving epithets or anaphoric descriptions (rather than anaphoric pronouns):

(7)   a. I met John$_i$/my new neighbour$_i$ the other day
      b. The bastard$_i$ did not greet me

Do we want to treat the name 'John' (or the description 'my new neighbour') and the anaphoric description 'the bastard' as (two tokens of) *the same expression type*? Aren't they, rather, two distinct expressions, despite being coindexed? Clearly they are. Yet the issue is more complex than meets the eye. According to a recent analysis, epithets like 'the bastard' in (7) actually are (null) *pronouns* modified by a nominal appositive (Patel-Grosz 2012). The logical form of (7b) would be:

(7b*)   *pro$_i$*, the bastard, did not greet me.

If this is right, then we could treat the null pronoun *pro$_i$* as the same syntactic expression as its antecedent, in Fiengo and May's sense, while acknowledging that the appositive description 'the bastard' is *not* the same expression as, e.g., the antecedent description 'my new neighbour'. (Indeed, the two descriptions carry distinct meanings.)

Be that as it may, we don't have to treat an anaphoric pronoun as the same expression as its antecedent to acknowledge that *recurrence* is what ultimately grounds coreference *de jure*. What recurs, arguably, is not (or not necessarily) a *linguistic* representation but a *mental* representation. Let us admit that 'in cases of anaphora (as when I say "I saw John, he was wearing a bowler hat"), we can have two expressions representing an object as the same without the expressions themselves being the same' (Fine 2007: 41). This does not prevent us from accepting Fiengo and May's point that there *is* identity, at a suitably deep level of analysis. There is, one might say, identity at the *conceptual* level—at the level of thought or logical form. The expressions 'John' and 'he' are not the same, in the ordinary sense of 'expression', but they are associated with the same conceptual representation, and that is what coindexing indicates. Because of coindexing, anyone who understands the utterance has to *redeploy* the singular concept associated with the name when processing the anaphoric pronoun. Likewise, in (7) the antecedent 'John' (or 'my new neighbour') and the anaphoric description 'the bastard' are associated with *the same singular representation*. Anyone who understands the utterance has to redeploy the singular concept associated with the antecedent when processing the anaphoric description.

Placing the relevant identity at the conceptual level does not mean that it is not syntactically encoded. Sentences partially encode thoughts, and it is plausible that *recurrence constraints on conceptual elements* are encoded in the syntax of natural language. What recurs, however, is primarily a conceptual element (whether or not there is identity of expression at the linguistic level). That justifies shifting focus to the mental level and considering the associated representations directly.

Another consideration supports the shift to the cognitive level. Arguably, there is nothing specifically *linguistic* about Trading on Identity, coordination, etc. Suppose I hold a glass in my hand while looking at it. The glass looks dirty, and it feels cold. When, on the basis of my perceptual experience, I judge that the glass is cold and dirty, I trade upon the identity of the seen glass and the touched glass (Campbell 1987). Similarly, when I keep track of the glass from t to t' and judge that it is moving, I trade upon the identity of the object I perceive at the various times throughout the attentional episode (Evans 1981). That is already, at the most basic level, the phenomenon we are trying to elucidate. In other words: when I say 'the glass$_1$ looks dirty, and it$_1$ feels cold', what I express in language is a thought whose constituents already bear the relevant relation of coreference *de jure* to each other. Likewise, when, on the basis of my perception of the glass, I form the intention to drink from it, there is coreference *de jure* between the referential elements in the perceptual judgment and the intention based on it (Kamp 1990). Coreference *de jure*, even though it manifests itself in language, is first and foremost a phenomenon at the level of thought.[7]

1.3. Mental Files

According to many authors in the recent singular thought literature, the singular concepts through which we represent particulars

---

[7] See Kamp 1990: 47. When it comes to thought, Fine talks of 'corepresentation' rather than 'coreference'.

(e.g. our concept of Cicero) are best construed as *mental files binding together the subject's predications concerning a given object*. Predications bound to the same file, being about the same object as a matter of representational architecture, are *eo ipso* 'coordinated' and license Trading on Identity. If there are two predicates *F* and *G* in the subject's file for a given individual (or in one of his files if he has several), the predicates are coordinated and the subject can infer that there is an *x* which is both *F* and *G*. But to get that result it is not sufficient for the subject to predicate *being F* and *being G* of one and the same object. If the subject predicates *F* and *G* of the same object by thinking of it through two distinct files (e.g. because she mistakenly thinks there are two distinct objects, Cicero and Tully, or because she takes the point of view of someone who does), then Trading on Identity is blocked. The subject cannot justifiably infer that there is an *x* which is both *F* and *G*.

I have just mentioned the case of a subject who mistakenly thinks there are two distinct objects while there is only one. That is a 'Frege case', illustrated by the Babylonians' thoughts about Hesperus and Phosphorus (Fodor 1995: 22–4). In such cases, it is possible for a rational subject to ascribe contradictory properties to the object since, from the subject's point of view, there are two distinct objects and no contradiction is internally detectable. Frege accounted for such cases by distinguishing sense from reference. The sense is the way the reference is presented—the 'mode of presentation'. In Frege cases, there is a single reference but two distinct modes of presentation.

That there are two distinct modes of presentation in Frege cases is definitive of modes of presentation. Nothing is a mode of presentation unless it obeys what Schiffer calls 'Frege's Constraint':

Necessarily, if *m* is a mode of presentation under which a minimally rational person *x* believes a thing *y* to be F, then it is not the case that *x* also believes *y* not to be F under *m*. In other words, if *x* believes *y* to be F and also believes *y* not to be F, then there are distinct modes of presentation m and m' such that x believes y to be F under m and disbelieves y to be F under m'. Let us call this *Frege's Constraint*; it is a constraint which any candidate must satisfy if it is to qualify as a mode of presentation.   (Schiffer 1978: 180)

Mental files satisfy the constraint, so they qualify as modes of presentation. Let us imagine a Babylonian, Hammurabi, who assertively entertains the thought that *Hesperus is visible in the evening but Phosphorus is not* (it is visible in the morning). He refers to Venus twice, by means of the singular terms 'Hesperus' and 'Phosphorus' which are associated, for him, with two distinct mental files. The two contradictory predications 'visible in the evening' (predicated of Hesperus) and 'not visible in the evening' (predicated of Phosphorus) are bound to distinct mental files and give rise to no contradiction within any of the two files. The contradiction remains internally undetectable, so the subject's rationality is not impugned. But if the singular terms were, in the subject's mind, associated with the same mental file, the two predications would be coordinated and the contradiction would be immediately apparent. Trading on Identity would be licensed, and the subject would have to face the conclusion that some object is both visible in the evening and not visible in the evening (a contradiction). A rational subject would therefore be led to retract one of the two contradictory predications. It follows that Frege's Constraint is satisfied: if x believes y to be F and also believes y not to be F, then there are distinct mental files m and m' such that x believes y to be F under m and disbelieves y to be F under m'.

In this framework, coreference *de jure* at the language level is to be accounted for in terms of deployment of the same file in thought. The identity which grounds coreference *de jure* is not the identity of the expressions but the identity of the mental file associated with them.

Note that, because they play the mode of presentation role, mental files must satisfy a transparency constraint: the subject must know when the same mental file is deployed twice, and when two distinct mental files are deployed. Transparency is what motivates the sense/reference distinction in the first place. The subject may not realize that two terms (e.g. 'Hesperus' and 'Phosphorus') refer to the same object, or that they refer to distinct objects. So reference is not epistemically transparent. In contrast, sense *must be* transparent. If modes of presentation are not transparent, there is no reason to move from pure referential talk to mode of presentation talk in the explanation of rational behaviour (e.g. the subject's assenting to 'Hesperus is visible in the evening' but not to 'Phosphorus is visible in the evening'). Sense is the level at which the subject's rationality can be assessed, and this entails that senses are transparent to the thinker.

2

Factivity, Transparency, and Weak Coreference De Jure

2.1. Factivity

WE started in Chapter 1 with a characterization of *de jure* coreference as a relation of coreference that holds in virtue of meaning. Because the coreference relation holds in virtue of meaning, whoever grasps the meaning knows that the relation obtains.[1] Coreference is guaranteed by meaning—by what the subject grasps—so it cannot fail to obtain. This corresponds to Fine's notion of *strict coreference*. Strict coreference is semantically required coreference—coreference that is required in virtue of one's semantic knowledge. Mere coreference is not enough: it must be part of the subject's semantic knowledge that there is coreference. Since knowledge is factive, strict coreference also is factive: if there is strict coreference between two singular terms M and N, there is *eo ipso* coreference between them.

---

[1] In taking coreference *de jure* to be a matter of knowledge, I follow Ángel Pinillos. A reader for Oxford University Press thinks this is a mistake, and suggests a weaker formulation that avoids crediting subjects with sophisticated beliefs about coreference relations. I respond to that objection in the Preface, note 2.

But there is a snag. Sometimes, two terms are coreferential *de jure* by the standard tests (the subject presupposes coreference and trades upon identity) while in fact there is no coreference. According to Lawlor (2010), the existence of such cases shows that Fine's notion of strict coreference is not the right notion to capture the phenomenon. The phenomenon we are after, she says, is *internal* coreference. It is, *for the subject*, a priori that the two terms corefer. Internal coreference is the idea that coreference is presupposed by the subject, but this does not entail actual coreference. Internal coreference is not factive, Lawlor argues. This suggests that we should get rid of the following claim, central to Fine's characterization of coreference *de jure* as strict coreference:

Factivity

Coreference *de jure* (in Fine's framework: strict coreference) entails coreference.

There are two types of case in which factivity seems to fail. First, there are empty singular terms. They do not refer, yet they can stand in *internal* 'coreferential' relations. Thus the subject can point to an object he hallucinates, attempt to designate it by, e.g., 'that dagger', and then attempt to *de jure* corefer to the same object by uttering an anaphoric pronoun 'it' or by uttering an anaphoric description 'the dagger'. In such a case the subject trades upon identity in the normal way and coordinates his predications (so there is 'coreference *de jure*', by the standard tests), yet the failure of reference prevents coreference relations from actually obtaining. (Coreference entails reference, so, by contraposition, non-reference entails non-coreference.) The same sort of thing happens when one uses fictional names in discourse: a fictional name and a pronoun anaphoric on it bear the same referential index (they are associated with the same mental file), so they are coreferential *de jure*, by the standard tests; yet, because neither of the singular term refers, they cannot corefer.

The second type of case in which factivity fails is the case in which the subject is confused. Lawlor gives the following example:

Wally says of Udo, 'He needs a haircut', and Zach, thinking to agree, but looking at another person, says, 'he sure does'. (Lawlor 2010: 4)

Here, Zach presupposes that, in his dialogue with Wally, the two occurrences of the pronoun 'he' corefer, but the presupposition is false. There is internal coreference for Zach since he trades upon the identity of the object he is looking at and the object antecedently referred to by Wally, but there is no actual coreference.

Fine agrees that internal coreference (what corresponds to the subject's own point of view) is not factive. The subject may treat two expressions as *de jure* coreferential, and behave accordingly (trading on identity, etc.), even though the terms do not actually corefer. However, rather than giving up his (factive) characterization of *de jure* coreference as 'strict coreference' (a notion which entails actual coreference), Fine maintains it and attempts to define (non-factive) internal coreference in terms of it. In other words, Fine advocates a view according to which there are *two distinct notions* of coreference *de jure* rather than a single one. Strict coreference corresponds to a first notion, that of semantically required coreference. That is the basic notion. Two terms are strictly coreferential just in case it is part of one's semantic knowledge that they corefer. Knowledge is factive, so strict coreference entails actual coreference. The other notion is that of internal or putative coreference, which corresponds to the subject's point of view. Fine analyses it in terms of the basic notion. There is internal or putative coreference between two terms just in case the subject *treats them as* strictly coreferential, i.e. takes it for granted that they are. In the problematic cases, the subject is mistaken. There is no actual coreference and, therefore, no strict reference either (since strict coreference entails coreference).

On Fine's picture, we must distinguish putative (or internal) coreference from strict coreference just as we distinguish strict coreference from mere *de facto* coreference. The three notions are built up as follows:

Mere (de facto) coreference: M and N corefer
    COREF (M, N).

Strict coreference: it is part of the subject's semantic knowledge that (or: it is a semantic requirement that) M and N corefer
    □ COREF (M, N).

Putative coreference: it is taken to be the case that M and N strictly corefer
    T □ COREF (M, N).

Strict coreference is factive, but putative coreference is not. Here is Fine's own gloss on the trio of notions:

Since the notion of being a semantic requirement is factive, the relation of strict coreference is likewise factive; strict coreference will imply coreference. And it is for this reason that the relation cannot be taken to be the relation of internal coreference. However, the notion of a putative semantic requirement is not factive; it can be a putative semantic requirement that P even though P is not the case. Suppose we take two singular terms to be putatively coreferential if it is a putative semantic requirement that they corefer. Then the relation of putative coreference is likewise not factive; two terms can putatively corefer without coreferring. And so there is no obstacle—or, at least, not the same obstacle—to taking this relation to be the relation of internal coreference in cases of confused reference.   (Fine 2010: 497)

For Fine, coreference *de jure* is strict coreference, but Trading on Identity (TI) is not a an infallible test. What TI shows is that the subject treats the two terms as coreferential *de jure* (strictly coreferential). That does not entail that they are. In cases of delusion and confusion, they are not.

The problem is that meaning is supposed to be transparent, i.e. known to the language users (Dummett 1978: 131). Since *de jure* coreferential relations are an aspect of meaning, it seems that they *must be* transparent to the language user. It must not be possible for the language user to be mistaken as to whether or not the relevant coreference relations hold. But that is exactly what Fine says is possible in the case of strict coreference: it is possible for the subject to take it that there is (strict) coreference while in fact there isn't. This suggests that strict coreference is the wrong foundation for an account of coreference *de jure*. It lacks the required sort of transparency.

2.2. 'Subjective' and 'Objective' Aspects of Coreference De Jure

Because of the factivity problem, Lawlor suggests *substituting* internal coreference for Fine's strict coreference in the analysis of coreference *de jure*. Internal coreference is not factive, in contrast to strict coreference; it can hold between two terms M and N even though M and N are not actually coreferential. Similarly, Pinillos rejects Fine's notion of strict (semantically required) coreference and posits a primitive relation between singular terms, 'p-linking', which is non-factive (Pinillos 2015: 324).

But I think one should not let factivity go too hastily. We are not interested in what the language users *take to be the case* (a non-factive notion), but in what they *know to be the case* in virtue of their linguistic understanding. As Fine rightly insists, what we are after is a *semantic fact*, corresponding to the relation of *de jure* coreference. We must distinguish that semantic fact (something objective) from the subjective state a person is in when she knows that fact—the CDJ state, as I call it:

CDJ state

A subject is in the CDJ state with respect to two expressions M and N just in case she presupposes coreference between M and N and is therefore disposed to 'trade on identity'.[2]

---

[2] The CDJ state corresponds to what Schroeter calls 'the appearance of *de jure* sameness', which she characterizes as 'the subjective appearance of obvious, incontrovertible and epistemically basic sameness of subject matter' (Schroeter 2012, §1).

Internal coreference (in the sense of Lawlor and Fine) holds between two terms just in case the subject is in the CDJ state with respect to them. Cases of emptiness and confusion show that a speaker may be in the CDJ state with respect to M and N even though M and N are not actually coreferential. *But that does not mean that the 'objective' notion of coreference de jure we are after is not itself factive.* There is, I claim, something which the speaker in the CDJ state (and anyone who understands the discourse) *knows* about the relation in which the two terms stand to each other. More precisely: there is a relation R such that, when the speaker is in the CDJ state with respect to a pair of terms M and N, he or she (and anyone who understands the discourse) knows that M and N stand in relation R. That relation R I call the *base relation* for *de jure* coreference. Coreference *de jure* is defined in terms of it:

Coreference de jure (schematic definition)

Two terms M and N are coreferential *de jure* = _{def} The speaker is in the CDJ state with respect to them and, as a result, anyone who properly understands the discourse knows that the base relation R obtains between M and N.[3]

Since coreference *de jure* involves knowledge, it is factive: whenever two terms M and N are coreferential *de jure*, they ipso facto bear the relation R to each other. Of course, I have not forgotten the counterexamples to factivity, based on emptiness or confusion. But they were only counterexamples to *a specific way of construing the base relation R.* The subject in the CDJ state cannot be said to 'know' that M and N are R-related, if we take R to be the plain coreference relation (a relation which may actually fail to hold);[4] but there are other, more secure candidates for the R relation than

---

[3] I am indebted to Jack Spencer for remarks that led me to this formulation, and to Ángel Pinillos for an argument in its favour.

[4] As we have seen, M and N can be *de jure* coreferential (by the standard tests) even though M and N do not corefer.

plain coreference. By suitably weakening the R relation, we can rescue factivity for coreference *de jure*.

What about transparency? In the mental file framework, coreference *de jure* is a matter of file identity, and the transparency of the R relation is guaranteed. An utterance is not understood unless the interpreter is able to associate the right modes of presentation with all the referential occurrences of expressions in the sentence. The right modes of presentation are mental files in the interpreter's mind, meeting the constraints imposed by the meaning of the sentence and the context, and coordinated with the speaker's own files, which are subject to the same constraints (Part II). Now, modes of presentation are transparent: the subject knows when the same mental file is deployed twice, and when two distinct mental files are deployed (Section 1.3). It follows that a competent and properly situated interpreter will associate mental files with all the referential expressions in the sentence and will know, for any two such files deployed in interpreting the utterance, whether or not they are occurrences of the same file. That means that, for any two referential expressions in the sentence, the competent and properly situated interpreter will know whether or not they are associated (in his/her mind) with the same file. If they are, the competent and properly situated interpreter will know that no referential divergence is possible between M and N. In other words, M and N will be *de jure* coreferential, and the base relation between M and N will be transparent to competent and properly situated interpreters.

2.3. *Weakening the Base Relation*

Fine himself (in passing) has mentioned different manners of construing the base coreference relation appealed to in the characterization of strict coreference. He writes the following in a footnote:

Coreference between the names N and M may be defined *existentially* as
∃x(Ref(N, x) & Ref(M, x)) or *universally* as ∀x(Ref(N, x) ≡ Ref(M, x)). The
two definitions are equivalent given that N and M have unique referents,
i.e. given ∃!xRef(N, x) & ∃!xRef(M, x). (. . .) However, *when empty names
are in question, it may be important to adopt the universal rather than the
existential form of definition, since it will then be possible to distinguish between
different empty names in regard to whether they strictly corefer.*   (Fine 2007:
134–5, emphasis mine)

The universal definition of coreference corresponds to Perry's
notion of *conditional coreference* or 'coco-reference'. Taylor's notion
of explicit coreference, Pinillos's notion of coreference *de jure*,
Fiengo and May's notion of grammatically determined coreference, Gibbard's notion of assumed coreference, Goodsell's notion
of IK-coreference, etc.—all work in the same way. In each case, the
relation holds provided the two singular terms corefer *if they
refer at all*. That conditional relation holds between the singular
terms even if they fail to refer (in which case the antecedent of
the conditional is false). This suggests the following characterization of coreference *de jure* as entailing knowledge of *conditional*
coreference:

Coreference de jure (conditional characterization)

The speaker is in the CDJ state with respect to two terms
M and N, and as a result, anyone who properly understands
the discourse knows that M and N corefer *if they refer at all.*

If we take the base coreference relation to be conditional
coreference, then we can accommodate the empty cases (hallu-
cination, fiction, etc.) without having to split coreference *de
jure* as Fine does when he distinguishes strict coreference and
internal/putative coreference. Under the conditional characterization, coreference *de jure* is factive. If M and N are coreferential *de
jure*, it is a semantic fact that they corefer if they refer at all. That
is true even if the terms are empty (in which case the antecedent
of the conditional is false), so there is no need to give up factivity

to dispose of the alleged counterexamples based on emptiness. When two singular terms are coreferential *de jure*, a competent and properly situated language user knows that they corefer if they refer at all, and that is compatible with the terms's failing to refer.

But there is the other class of counterexamples—the cases of *referential confusion*, as in the Zach/Wally story, repeated here:

Wally says of Udo, 'He needs a haircut', and Zach, thinking to agree, but looking at another person, says, 'he sure does'.   (Lawlor 2010: 4)

In such a case, it seems that *even conditional coreference fails*. One cannot say that the two singular terms (the two pronouns) corefer if they refer at all. Certainly, the pronoun in Wally's mouth does refer (it refers to Udo). But it is implausible that the second pronoun (in Zach's mouth) also refers to Udo. Clearly, Zach is confused: he purports to refer not to Udo, but to another person he sees, whom he wrongly takes to be the person Wally was referring to. We can say either that Zach refers to that other person he sees, or, preferably in my view, that he fails to refer because he is confusedly tracking two distinct objects at the same time (namely the person he sees and the person Wally initially referred to). Whichever option we pick, the conditional coreference requirement is falsified: it is not the case that:

$$\forall x(\text{Ref}(\text{`he'}_{\text{Wally}}, x) \equiv \text{Ref}(\text{`he'}_{\text{Zach}}, x))$$

where 'he'$_{\text{Wally}}$ and 'he'$_{\text{Zach}}$ refer to the tokens of the pronoun 'he' in Zally's mouth and Zach's respectively. It is because of such cases that we seem compelled to give up factivity and make room for a non-factive notion of coreference *de jure*.

One might legitimately discard that type of example on the grounds that it involves a *dialogue*. The two singular terms that are supposed to be coreferential *de jure* belong to the utterances of two distinct persons. Such cases introduce considerable complications, as two different points of view (and the mental files of two different subjects) come into play.[5] However, there are *other* examples of confusion which have the same structure but do not involve a dialogue. Some examples, such as the following, do not even involve language.

Imagine a subject who continuously tracks an object as it moves. At some point, unbeknown to the subject, a substitution occurs. The initial object, A, is replaced by a different object, B. Before the substitution, the subject's thought is about A. After the substitution, the subject's thought seems to be about B (the new object). Presupposing the identity of the object B he is now tracking ('that is F') and the object A he was tracking before the substitution ('that was G a moment ago'), the subject trades upon the identity and infers: 'something which was G a moment ago is now F'. If this description of the case is correct, the subject is in the CDJ state with respect to the two demonstratives even though they refer to different things. So it is not true that the subject in the CDJ state with respect to two terms M and N knows that they corefer if they refer at all. In the confusion cases, the condition 'M and N corefer if they refer' is not satisfied (either the terms refer to different things, or one of the terms refers while the other doesn't), so it cannot be 'known'.

To dispose of the counterexamples, one may point out that in some of the confusion cases at least, the subject (e.g. Zach in Lawlor's example) is not a 'competent and properly situated' language user. Emptiness can never be ruled out, even if the subject is fully competent, but confusion is a different beast: it betrays a lack of understanding. Now, according to the conditional characterization, M and N are coreferential *de jure* only if *whoever properly understands the discourse knows that they corefer if they refer at all.* In the confusion cases that necessary condition is apparently not satisfied: the subject is in the CDJ state with respect to M and N yet she does not 'know' that they corefer if they refer. This, however, is not a genuine

---

[5] See Chapter 3 for discussion of such cases.

counterexample to the conditional characterization since the confused subject does not 'properly understand the discourse'.

The problem with this way of handling the confusion cases is that it does not generalize. It is true that Zach is confused and does not properly understand Wally's utterance. In his interpretation of Wally's utterance, Zach is making a mistake. But there are also cases of *innocent confusion*, i.e. cases in which the subject is confused not because of any mistake on his or her part, but because *the world fails to cooperate*.[6] Thus, in the non-linguistic example I have presented (the demonstrative tracking case with hidden substitution), the subject is blameless: the substitution that occurred, perhaps due to the operation of a Cartesian evil genius, is not the sort of thing that the subject can be expected to anticipate.

Confronted with counterexamples based on (possibly innocent) confusion, there is another strategy we can use, namely, the same strategy we used to rescue factivity in the face of the empty cases. In the empty cases, what makes it possible to retain factivity is a shift in the base coreference relation in terms of which coreference *de jure* is defined. Instead of taking the base coreference relation to be the relation which holds between two terms just in case *there is* an object to which they both refer ($\exists$-coreference), we take it to be that which holds between two terms whenever *any* object to which one of the terms refers is also referred to by the other term ($\forall$-coreference). That base coreference relation is universal, not existential. Coreference *de jure* based on that coreference relation is compatible with failure of reference, so it can do the work of internal coreference when the terms are both empty. The subject in the CDJ state with respect to two terms M and N which turn out to be empty is still correct in treating the two terms as coreferential in the base sense, that is, as such that *if* one term refers to a certain object then the other term does as well. The idea, then, is to appeal to the same strategy in dealing with the cases of confusion, by weakening the base relation once again.

[6] See the quotation from Millikan in the Preface, note 5.

2.4. *Weak Coreference* De Jure

So far we have two candidates for the base relation R between two singular terms M and N in a situation of coreference *de jure*:

- The $\exists$-coreference relation: $\exists x(\text{Ref}(N, x) \ \& \ \text{Ref}(M, x))$
- The $\forall$-coreference relation: $\forall x(\text{Ref}(N, x) \equiv \text{Ref}(M, x))$

If we choose to base coreference *de jure* on the $\exists$-coreference relation, we cannot maintain factivity for coreference *de jure* because of both empty cases and cases of confusion. If we choose to base coreference *de jure* on the $\forall$-coreference relation, we can account for empty cases without giving up factivity, but cases of confusion are still counterexamples. To deal with these cases, we have to shift to an *even weaker* base relation. At this point, it will help to consider all the possible coreference options for two singular terms M and N.

There are four main types of (non-)coreference relation between M and N in a given piece of discourse (Table 2.1). Cases of type 1 corresponds to the $\exists$-coreference relation. If we base coreference *de jure* on that relation, we cannot account for cases of type 2 to 4 consistently with factivity. The $\forall$-coreference relation does better since it covers both cases of type 1 ($\exists$-coreference) *and* cases of type 2 (the empty cases), but the notion of coreference *de jure* based on that relation still cannot be factive because of the possibility of cases of referential divergence (type 3 or 4) and not merely of referential emptiness.

Table 2.1. Possible coreference relations between two singular terms M and N

Type 1. The two terms refer to the same object
Type 2. The two terms fail to refer
Type 3. One term refers to something, the other term fails to refer
Type 4. One term refers to something, the other term refers to something else

---

To accommodate (some of) the cases involving referential divergence, we can weaken the base relation a little more, by *reinterpreting* the claim that two terms are coreferential *de jure* only if they are known to *corefer if they refer at all*. For that claim is ambiguous: the conditional coreference relation ('corefer if they refer') can be interpreted in two ways, only one of which corresponds to $\forall$-coreference. The two interpretations are:

- *Conditional coreference (strong)*: M and N corefer if *either* refers (= $\forall$-coreference).
- *Conditional coreference (weak)*: M and N corefer if *both* refer.

These two base relations give us two alternative notions of coreference *de jure*, a weak one ('weak CDJ') and a strong one ('strong CDJ'):[7]

Strong CDJ

The speaker is in the CDJ state with respect to two terms M and N, and as a result, anyone who properly understands the discourse knows that *M and N corefer if either refers*.

Weak CDJ

The speaker is in the CDJ state with respect to two terms M and N, and as a result, anyone who properly understands the discourse knows that *M and N corefer if both refer*.

According to the *strong* notion of coreference *de jure*, a subject in the CDJ state with respect to M and N knows that:

$$\forall x(\mathrm{Ref}(N, x) \equiv \mathrm{Ref}(M, x)).$$

This rules out all cases of referential divergence between M and N, whether of type 3 or of type 4 (Table 2.1). If there are such cases,

---

[7] In Chapter 3, we shall see that there are not merely two distinct *notions* of coreference *de jure* (the weak one and the strong one), but two distinct phenomena—two distinct *forms* of coreference *de jure*.

strong CDJ is not what we need. Now it seems that a subject *can* be in the CDJ state with respect to M and N even though, because of confusion, one of the two terms (but not the other) fails to refer. Thus Wally's use of the pronoun 'he' refers to Udo, while Zach's partly anaphoric use of the pronoun 'he' is confused. Zach's pronoun is linked deictically to the person he sees and anaphorically to Wally's pronoun (since Zach wrongly assumes that the person he sees is the person Wally was referring to). To the extent that Zach's pronoun targets two different individuals, it fails to refer, contrary to Wally's pronoun. Still, Zach is in the CDJ state with respect to the two pronouns, so we want to say that there *is* coreference *de jure* between them; but this is only possible (consistently with factivity) if we give the *weak* interpretation of coreference *de jure*. Only weak CDJ allows for cases in which *one of the term refers and the other one fails to refer* (type 3). With respect to such cases, the analysis of coreference *de jure* as strong CDJ would violate the factivity constraint. Factivity can be restored, however, by moving to weak CDJ. Weak CDJ is based on a relation R weaker than the $\forall$-coreference relation.[8]

According to the weak characterization of coreference *de jure*, a subject in the CDJ state with respect to M and N knows that if *both* terms refer, then they refer to the same thing. That is our third candidate for the status of base relation:

- The $\forall\forall$-coreference relation: $\forall x \forall y \, ((\mathrm{Ref}(\mathrm{N}, x) \ \& \ \mathrm{Ref}(\mathrm{M}, y)) \rightarrow \mathrm{x} = \mathrm{y})$.

---

[8] Weak CDJ corresponds to what philosophers generally mean by 'coreference *de jure*'. Thus Pinillos says that a fully competent subject knows, of two occurrences M and N that are *de jure* coreferential, that they 'refer to the same object if the first refers to some object and the second refers to some object'; they 'know of the expression occurrences that that if both have referents, then they refer to the same thing' (Pinillos 2011: 304; see also Pinillos 2015: 325). Goodsell's 2014 account of *de jure* coreference also equates it with weak CDJ: see her definition of 'IK-coreference' (Goodsell 2014: 309). Drapeau Vieira Contim (2016) is an exception: coreference *de jure*, for him, is strong CDJ, based on the $\forall$-coreference relation (see his principle of 'referential equivalence').

The ∀∀-coreference relation covers not only cases of emptiness but also cases of confusion (type 3), since in such cases the antecedent of the conditional is false: it is not the case that the two terms refer (since one of them fails to refer). Factivity is rescued, because the conditional is true, in such circumstances. If M and N are *de jure* coreferential (in the weak sense), then, whether or not the subject is deluded or confused, it is a fact that M and N corefer if they both refer.

2.5. *Type-4 Cases*

Even weak CDJ rules out cases of type 4, i.e. cases in which M and N *refer to two different things* (strong referential divergence). Referential divergence is only allowed if one of the two terms fails to refer (while the other succeeds in referring to some object). When one of the terms fails to refer, the antecedent of the conditional ('if both refer') is falsified, so the conditional itself ('corefer if they both refer') remains true. This is consistent with factivity. But in a case of type 4, both M and N refer (so the antecedent is true) yet they do not corefer—they refer to two distinct things. How can we dispose of such counterexamples? Can we weaken the base relation even more to accommodate cases of strong referential divergence?

Fortunately, we do not have to (or so I claim). Type 4 is not a problem, because there are no examples in which the subject is in the CDJ state with respect to two terms M and N yet M and N straightforwardly refer to distinct things. Cases of confusion arguably fall either under type 2 or under type 3, but never under type 4. The reason is plain: *if the subject is confused, at least one of the two singular terms must fail to refer*. If I am right, there is no need to worry about type 4.

To be sure, many people have the intuition that, e.g., Zach in Lawlor's example does refer to the person he is looking at when he says 'He sure does', despite Zach's mistaken belief that that person is the person Wally was referring to when he said 'He needs a haircut'. That intuition seems to support the existence of type-4 cases of confusion. But I think the intuition can be accounted for consistently with my take on the non-existence of type-4 cases.

What we need is a notion of *partial* reference (distinguished from reference *simpliciter*) such as that put forward by Field (1973) and used by Devitt (1981, 2015). In Lawlor's example, Wally unequivocally refers to Udo, but Zach is confused: through his use of the pronoun, Zach *partly* refers to the person he is looking at and *partly* to the person Wally was talking about. Zach's pronoun is linked deictically to the person he sees and anaphorically to Wally's pronoun. To the extent that Zach's pronoun targets two different individuals, it fails to refer *simpliciter*, contrary to Wally's pronoun. That is my claim. Still, there is a sense in which Zach does 'refer' to the person he is looking at—but that is only *partial* reference. In this framework, inspired by supervaluation theory, there is reference *simpliciter* only if *all* partial references converge on the same object, which is not the case in Lawlor's example. So Zach fails to refer *simpliciter*, even though he manages to *partially* refer to the person he is looking at. (I will have to say more about partial reference shortly.)

Now consider the non-linguistic example putatively of type 4 I described in Section 2.3. The subject tracks an object A as it moves but, at some point, a substitution of object B for object A occurs (unbeknown to the subject). Before the substitution, the subject's thought is uncontroversially about A. After the substitution, one might think that the subject's thought is about B (the new object). If it is, then the example falls under type 4. Presupposing the identity of the object B he is now tracking ('that is F') and the object A he was tracking before the substitution ('that was G a moment ago'), the subject trades upon the identity and infers: 'something which was G a moment ago is now F'. If this description of the case is correct, the subject is in the CDJ state with respect to the two demonstratives even though they refer to different things. But this description neglects the fact that, after the substitution (but not before), the subject's thought is confused. Before the substitution, the subject's thought is about A. After the substitution, it is (partially) about B, *but it continues to be (partially) about A*, because it is presupposed that a single object is being tracked throughout the attentional episode. The presupposition is false and, as a result, the subject's attempted demonstrative reference to 'the' object arguably fails (to some extent at least). This is a case of type 3—the sort of case which the weak notion of coreference *de jure* allows.

The partial reference framework allows us to go quantitative and achieve more fine-grainedness if we want to, by assigning *weights* to each partial reference. If Zach's use of the pronoun is (say) 30 per cent anaphoric and 70 per cent deictic, we'll have the intuition that Zach succeeds in referring to the person he is looking at, despite the confusion. If Zach's pronoun is 50 per cent anaphoric and 50 per cent deictic, we'll have the intuition that he fails to refer. We can accommodate these intuitions, while maintaining that in cases of confusion the speaker fails to refer *simpliciter* (because he partially refers to both x and y, where $x \neq y$). To achieve that result, we only have to pair the absolute notion of 'failure to refer' with a scale of pragmatic ignorability.[9] The greater the difference between the weight of the dominant demonstrative component and that of the anaphoric component, the more innocuous and pragmatically ignorable the failure of reference will be.

At this point, it may seem that I have conceded too much and that the ban on type-4 cases cannot be maintained. I have accepted that if Zach's use of the pronoun is 70 per cent deictic, the reference failure occasioned by the conflicting anaphoric link will be pragmatically ignorable. But if that is so, then it is easy to define a (pragmatically permissive) notion of reference such that Zach

9 On pragmatic ignorability, see Lasersohn 1999.

succeeds in referring to the person he is looking at (despite the anaphoric link to the person Wally was talking about). Is that not a type-4 case? In the pragmatically permissive sense of reference, Wally refers to Udo, Zach refers to the person he is looking at, and there is an anaphoric link between Zach's pronoun and Wally's!

But I think the ban on type-4 cases can be maintained, even if we opt for a pragmatically permissive notion of reference. In Lawlor's example, the demonstrative link underlying the use of Zach's pronoun can be dominant *only if* the anaphoric link also underlying it is correspondingly degraded. But the anaphoric link cannot be degraded without weakening the CDJ state. In the partial reference framework, everything becomes graded, including the strength of the CDJ state, so the ban on type-4 cases itself has to be reformulated in a graded manner. The following is a first approximation: *to the extent that the subject is in the CDJ state* with respect to two terms M and N, M and N cannot refer to two distinct objects.

3

Transitivity and Strong Coreference De Jure

3.1. Alleged Counterexamples to Transitivity

ACCOUNTING for coreference *de jure* in terms of identity of file entails that coreference *de jure* is a transitive relation (since identity is). But it is controversial whether coreference *de jure* is actually transitive, and there is an ongoing debate over precisely that issue (Pinillos 2011, Recanati 2012, Goodsell 2014, Drapeau Vieira Contim 2016).

Soames (1994: 253, 2009: 114) was the first to provide examples in which transitivity seems to fail:

(1)   Mary told *John* that *he* wasn't John

(2)   *John* fooled Mary into thinking that *he* was not John.

Let us focus on example (2). Transitivity seems to fail, for the following reason. We have seen that an anaphoric pronoun is coreferential *de jure* with its antecedent, so the first occurrence of 'John' in (2) is coreferential *de jure* with the pronoun 'he'. We have seen also that, in the normal course of events, two occurrences of the same proper name are coreferential *de jure*, so the first and the second occurrence of 'John' in (2) should be coreferential *de jure*. But the pronoun 'he' and the *second* occurrence of 'John' do not seem to be coreferential *de jure*. Frege's Constraint requires the existence of two distinct modes of presentation (distinct files) m and m' associated with the pronoun and the second occurrence of the name. Mary is said to have been fooled into thinking that John was not John. If Mary is rational, she must have thought of John under two distinct modes of presentation. But if there are two distinct modes of presentation, as in Frege cases, then the singular terms associated with these modes of presentation *cannot* be coreferential *de jure*. They can only be coreferential *de facto* (so the argument goes).

According to Soames, we should allow 'the term occurrences in the complement of (2) [to] be coordinated with the subject of "fooled" without being coordinated with each other' (Soames 2010: 474n). Since 'coordination' is another name for coreference *de jure*, Soames's proposal amounts to the claim that A can be coreferential *de jure* with B and B with C, *without* A's being coreferential *de jure* with C. But if we accept that coreference *de jure* is not transitive, then, Pinillos (2011) points out, we can no longer claim that we can account for it by associating mental files with singular terms. We can no longer say that what accounts for Trading on Identity is the fact that *the same file* is deployed twice. If coreference *de jure* was a matter of identity (of files, of senses, or of whatever) it would be transitive—but it is not. That is an argument against *all* the 'third object' views, which account for the phenomenon of coreference *de jure* by positing a single entity associated with the two singular terms.

The argument is not compelling, however. In the Soames example (and several others constructed by Pinillos on the same pattern), the failure of transitivity is merely apparent. The appearance is due to a shift in point of view. From the speaker's point of view (or more generally, from the point of view of the speech participants), the pronoun and the second occurrence of the name (that which does not serve as antecedent to the pronoun) *are* coreferential *de jure*. The same mental file for John is deployed in association with the first occurrence of the name, the pronoun, *and* the second occurrence of the name. The speaker and the understanding hearer know that it is *John* who fooled Mary into thinking that *he* was not *himself*. The appearance that there is only coreference *de facto* between the pronoun and the second occurrence of the name comes from the illegitimate intrusion of another point of view, that of Mary, the person to whom an attitude is ascribed in (2). Being rational, Mary must think of John under two distinct modes of presentation (via distinct mental files) in order to believe of him that he is not John. So the pronoun and the second occurrence of the name correspond, in Mary's thought, to two distinct ways of thinking of John. But this pertains to *Mary's thought*, not to the utterance. The mental files directly relevant to the interpretation of the utterance are those which *the speaker and her addressee* (and anyone who understands the utterance) associate with the singular terms. Mary's mental files are relevant only indirectly, because the utterance happens to report Mary's thoughts. (We shall see later that there are cases of 'oblique' reference in which the mental files of the ascribee are directly relevant to the interpretation of the singular terms; but that is not the case in this example.)

In *Direct Reference* (Recanati 1993), I drew a distinction between two types of mode of presentation at work in singular attitude ascriptions. In a singular attitude ascription, a thought is ascribed to someone, about a particular object. The speaker refers to the object in reporting a thought about it. The way the speaker (and his addressee) think of the object is the 'exercised mode of presentation'. The exercised mode of presentation is the way the reference is presented in the discourse—the files which the speaker and the hearer deploy in mentally relating to the object the discourse is about. A certain way of thinking of the object is typically also *ascribed*, in a context-dependent and tacit manner, to the person whose thought is reported. Unsurprisingly, that is what I call the 'ascribed mode of presentation'. Now the fact that, *in the ascribee's thought*, there are two distinct modes of presentation of the object (e.g. John, in Soames's example) does not establish that *the speaker* also deploys/exercises distinct modes of presentation in referring to that object. The distinctness of the modes of presentation in the ascribed thought (Mary's) is compatible with the uniqueness of the mode of presentation associated with the two name-occurrences and the pronoun anaphoric on one of them. Soames's examples, therefore, are compatible with the mental file account of coreference *de jure*, appearances notwithstanding. The files which matter when it comes to appraising whether or not two singular terms are associated with the same file are the files which the *speech protagonists* (not the characters whose thoughts are reported) deploy in referring to the objects the reported thoughts are about. They are the 'exercised modes of presentation'.

3.2. *Oblique Reference*

Sometimes, however, the mental files of some person distinct from the speaker, possibly the ascribee, are directly relevant to the interpretation of the singular terms and cannot be ignored by the theorist. Sometimes the speech protagonists *themselves* represent the object vicariously, via some file borrowed from some other person. This is a form of cognitive 'deference'. Think of identity statements like 'Hesperus is Phosphorus'. The speaker who says that, knows that Hesperus and Phosphorus are a single planet, but what she says is not the same thing as what she would say if she used the reflexive: 'Hesperus is itself' (Safir 1998: 141). Even though the speaker knows the identity and thinks of Hesperus/ Phosphorus as a single planet (Venus), the files which the speaker deploys in her thought and speech are not two deployments of her inclusive Venus file, but deployments of two distinct files, the Hesperus file and the Phosphorus file, which *correspond to the files in the mind of the subject who does not know the identity* (the hearer, perhaps).[1] As Laura Schroeter insightfully writes, an identity statement 'is best understood as responding to a doubt about the identity' of the individuals who are said to be the same (Schroeter 2007: 614n). In the Hesperus/Phosphorus case, the two singular terms are associated with the files through which the *unenlightened* thinks of Venus *qua* morning star and *qua* evening star. In such cases I say that there is *oblique reference*: the speaker refers to an object by deploying files 'indexed' to other people (by taking their point of view). The exercised mode of presentation, in such a case, is not a 'regular file' of the speaker's but a vicarious file indexed to some other subject whose point of view the speaker temporarily espouses[2] (on indexed files, see Recanati 2012: chapters 14 and 15).

Oblique reference may target a third party rather than the hearer. The possibility of deploying files indexed to third parties in referring is illustrated by my old 'your sister' example (Recanati 1987: 63). The speaker ironically says *'your sister' is coming over* and refers, by the description 'your sister' in quotes, to the person whom a third party takes to be the addressee's sister (but whom both the speaker and his addressee know not to be the addressee's sister). The file that is deployed in this case is a file about that person, containing the mistaken bit of information (that she is the addressee's sister). That file is indexed to the person the speaker is ironically mocking (the third party). It is not a 'regular file' in the mind of the speaker or the hearer, but a vicarious file used for essentially metarepresentational purposes (to represent how other people represent things in the common environment).

In the 'Hesperus is Phosphorus' case (and in identity statements more generally), the enlightened speaker deploys files indexed to the unenlightened addressee, and refers obliquely (to Venus)

---

[1] See Fiengo and May (2006: 152–3).
[2] Technically, there is no 'ascribed mode of presentation' in such an example, since it is not an attitude ascription. The same consideration applies to the next example of oblique reference (the 'sister' example). See Recanati 2012: 201–2.

through them. In a variant of that example, due to Pinillos, the target of oblique reference, i.e. the person to whom the vicarious files are indexed, is not the addressee but the speaker herself at an earlier time when she and her peers were not yet enlightened:

(3)   We were debating whether to investigate both *Hesperus* and *Phosphorus*; but when we got evidence of their true identity, we immediately sent probes *there*.

In the first clause the speaker espouses the point of view of the unenlightened (including herself before learning the identity), and she refers to Venus via two distinct mental files rather than via a single inclusive file corresponding to her current point of view. The inclusive file is associated with the demonstrative adverb 'there' at the end of the second clause. Again, the second clause expresses the subject's current point of view while the first clause is phrased from the point of view of the speaker and her peers before they learnt the identity. Since the first clause is a report ascribing certain speech acts to the speaker and her peers ('we were debating whether...'), the target of oblique reference in this case is the ascribee: the *exercised mode of presentation* associated with the two singular terms 'Hesperus' and 'Phosphorus' are mental files *indexed to the ascribee*, i.e. the speaker and her peers at the time of the deliberation which is reported.[3]

To sum up, Pinillos's example involves three coreferential files: two indexed files (the HESPERUS file and the PHOSPHORUS file, indexed to the ascribee) and a regular file (the inclusive VENUS file, corresponding to the speaker's current point of view). They all have the status of 'exercised mode of presentation' because the speaker deploys each of them in referring, so they cannot be discarded as irrelevant, as the ascribed modes of presentation were in discussing Soames's example.

---

[3] In this special case, the indexed files play the role of *both* exercised and ascribed modes of presentation.

Because they are associated with distinct files, it is doubtful that the terms 'Hesperus' and 'Phosphorus' in Pinillos's example are coreferential *de jure*. Indeed, the usual test shows that they are coreferential only *de facto*: someone who disbelieves the identity could still understand the first clause. In contrast, someone who disbelieves the identity would have trouble understanding the second clause, where the locative adverb 'there' can only refer if the identity 'Hesperus = Phosphorus' is true. As I said already, that adverb in the second clause is associated with the speaker's inclusive file for Venus. While the first clause is phrased from the point of view of the unenlightened (before learning the identity), the second clause reflects the point of view of the enlightened, after discovering the identity and opening an inclusive file.

The problem is that, even though the terms 'Hesperus' and 'Phosphorus' are only coreferential *de facto* in (3), *each of them is coreferential de jure with the inclusive term 'there' in the second clause* (the term associated with the inclusive file): the speech protagonists know that either 'there' fails to refer to a unique location (if the identity Hesperus = Phosphorus is not true), or (if the identity is true) it refers to the location of the single planet which Hesperus and Phosphorus turn out to be. That piece of knowledge corresponds to weak CDJ: for each of the two terms 'Hesperus' and 'Phosphorus', the subject knows that *that term corefers with the inclusive term 'there' if they both refer*. In other words: 'Hesperus' is in the (weak) CDJ relation to 'there', 'Phosphorus' is in the (weak) CDJ relation to 'there', yet 'Hesperus' and 'Phosphorus' do not stand in the weak CDJ relation to each other: they are not coreferential *de jure*, but *de facto*. This, Pinillos argues, shows that coreference *de jure* is not transitive. The proper representation of example (3), with coindexing, is:

(4)   We were debating whether to investigate both Hesperus$_1$ and Phosphorus$_2$; but when we got evidence of their true identity, we immediately sent probes there$_{1,2}$.

Pinillos gives another, particularly interesting variant of the example:

(5)   Hesperus$_1$ is Phosphorus$_2$ after all, so Hesperus-slash-Phosphorus$_{1,2}$ must be a very rich planet.

In the first clause, the speaker espouses the point of view of the unenlightened and deploys the HESPERUS and PHOSPHORUS files. In the second clause the speaker shifts to her current, enlightened point of view, and deploys the inclusive file. So far, this is like the previous example, but what is interesting about this variant is the term which is associated with the inclusive file in the second clause: 'Hesperus/Phosphorus'. That is a complex term, sometimes referred to as a 'slash-term'. Slash-terms are composed of two terms (the 'basic terms', here 'Hesperus' and 'Phosphorus') plus the slash operator.[4] What the slash operator does is create a new term which refers to the same thing as each of the basic terms if they corefer, and to nothing otherwise. The slash-term presupposes that the basic terms corefer, and itself refers only if the basic terms do corefer. It follows that *weak CDJ to each of the basic terms is a built-in feature of slash-terms*. Anyone who masters the slash-term knows a priori that either it corefers with each of the basic terms or it fails to refer. That is sufficient to support weak CDJ between the slash-term and each of the basic terms. Since the basic terms are only coreferential *de facto*, transitivity fails for weak CDJ: the two basic terms A and B are each coreferential *de jure* with the slash-term A/B, yet A and B themselves are not coreferential *de jure*.

In *Mental Files* (Recanati 2012), I acknowledged the failure of transitivity, and I weakened the theory accordingly. The Pinillos examples reveal that, for two terms to stand in the weak CDJ relation, it is not necessary for them to be associated with the same file. Two terms will also stand in the weak CDJ relation if one is associated with an initial file, and the other with an inclusive file

---

[4] The label 'basic term' comes from Drapeau Vieira Contim (2016).

resulting from the *fusion* of that initial file with another initial file presupposed to be coreferential with it. Being associated with the same file is therefore a sufficient condition for two terms to be coreferential *de jure*, but it is not a necessary condition.

I still accept what I said in *Mental Files*, but I think we should pay more attention to the distinction between weak CDJ and strong CDJ, construed now as two *forms* of coreference *de jure* (rather than two competing *conceptions* of what coreference *de jure* is). Weak CDJ, I maintain, is not transitive, and it cannot be equated to the relation of being associated with the same file (that would make it transitive, as Pinillos points out). Being associated with the same file is a sufficient condition for weak CDJ between two terms, but not a necessary condition. But I would like to suggest that strong CDJ *is* transitive, and *can* be equated to the relation of being associated with the same file. So we don't really need to weaken the theory (as I did in *Mental Files*), we only need to distinguish carefully between the two forms of coreference *de jure*, weak and strong.

3.3. *Confusion: The Diachronic Dimension*

We moved from strong CDJ (based on ∀-coreference) to weak CDJ (based on ∀∀-coreference) because of cases of confusion. The first case of confusion we encountered was the Zach–Wally case due to Lawlor. The subject is in the CDJ state with respect to the two utterances of 'he', yet the first occurrence refers to Udo while the second one, being based on confusion, fails to refer (it simultaneously tracks Udo and the person Zach is seeing). Wally utters the first 'he', and refers to Udo. Zach utters the second 'he', referring to the man he sees, who he wrongly takes to be the person Wally was referring to. Zach's utterance of 'he' is both deictic and anaphoric, it seems. The direct referential link to the person seen does not prevent Zach's pronoun from being anaphorically linked to Wally's: that is made possible by Zach's presupposition that Wally's referent is the person Zach sees. This was presented as a 'type 3 case', i.e. a case in which one term (Wally's 'he') refers to one thing (Udo), while the other term (Zach's 'he') fails to refer due to confusion (Section 2.3). But that example raises difficulties of its own, due to the fact that it involves a dialogue: the two occurrences of the pronoun 'he' that are supposed to be coreferential *de jure* are not uttered by the same person. Wally, indeed, refers to Udo, but *Zach takes Wally's pronoun to refer to the man he sees*, and it is with the pronoun *thus construed* that Zach intends to corefer *de jure*. If we consider only Zach's point of view, the mental file *he* associates with Wally's utterance of 'he' is the same mental file he associates with his own utterance of 'he', namely the confused file resulting from his mistaken identity presupposition.[5] It follows that, *from Zach's point of view*, the two pronouns corefer *de jure* in the strong sense: they corefer if either refers.

In Chapter 2, I said there were other 'type 3' examples, not involving a dialogue but exhibiting the same structure as the Zach–Wally example. In Section 2.4, I mentioned one that does not involve language at all. From time t_1 to t_3, the subject tracks an object as it moves, but fails to detect a substitution occurring at t_2, in the midst of the tracking episode. Before t_2, the subject's demonstrative file refers to A, the object tracked between t_1 and t_2. The object tracked between t_2 and t_3 is B, not A, but the file rests on the presupposition that one and the same object is being tracked throughout the attentional episode. Borrowing an idea from Hartry Field, I said that the file after t_2 partially refers to B and partially refers to A. A deployment of the file before t_2 therefore refers to A, while a deployment of the 'same' file after t_2 refers to both A and B and so fails to refer *simpliciter*, the world failing to cooperate. In such a case, as in the more spectacular cases of mistaken fusion of files (e.g. Marco Polo's confusion regarding Madagascar), the weak

---

[5] I am indebted to Philippe Lusson here.

CDJ relation holds between the initial file (before t_2) and the more inclusive file deployed after t_2.[6] I describe the file after t_2 as 'more inclusive' because it stores information from both A and B, and it rests on more information channels (the subject after t_2 remembers how 'the object' was before while perceiving how 'it' now is).

Because, in that example, the inclusive file presupposes the identity of the object tracked between t_1 and t_2 and the object tracked between t_2 and t_3, the structure of the example is similar to that of Strawson's cases of 'merging'. According to Strawson (1974), when one learns an identity, one merges the files one initially had. The inclusive file resulting from merging the two initial files rests on a presupposition of identity (it is, in Drapeau Vieira Contim's terms, 'identity-dependent'). If the identity fails to hold, the inclusive file (and the slash-term possibly associated with it) fails to refer, but that does not prevent each of the initial files from referring. Both the infelicitous tracking case and the mistaken merge case are of 'type 3', the type of case that justifies moving from strong CDJ to weak CDJ.

Another type of example with the same structure involves mistaken recognition. One remembers a certain object A, and upon encountering an object B wrongly recognizes it as A. The initial memory file is about A, while the post-recognition file mixes memory information about A and perceptual information about B, presupposing that A and B are the same. This is an instance of what I call 'incremental conversion' (Recanati 2012, 2013a): a file grows new information links as time passes, and its continued existence rests on the presupposition that all the information derives from the same object. If the identity presupposition is false, that is, in this case, if A $\neq$ B, the initial memory file and the more inclusive recognitional file (hosting information derived from both memory

---

⁶ When I speak of the weak CDJ relation as holding between two files (rather than between terms), I mean that the subject who deploys the files knows that they corefer if both refer.

and current perception) diverge in their referential status: the initial memory file refers to A, while its post-recognitional continuation fails to refer, due to confusion. Even though they are, in a dynamic sense, the 'same file', they are better seen as two distinct *file-stages* with divergent referential fates: the memory file before t_2 refers to A, while the inclusive file after t_2 fails to refer. Whenever that structure is instantiated, strong CDJ fails: it is not true that the two files 'refer if either refers'. One refers, but the other doesn't. Rather, the two files stand in the weak CDJ relation: although the identity presupposition is mistaken, the subject in the CDJ state still knows that the two files corefer if they both refer.

It is worth noting that, in all these non-linguistic examples of confusion, the files in the weak CDJ relation are *deployed at different times*. Merging is the process through which an inclusive file substitutes for two initial files, which Strawson describes as 'withdrawn' (Strawson 1974: 56). Likewise, the recognitional file supersedes the memory file, and the demonstrative file after t_2 supersedes the earlier file-stage (the demonstrative file before t_2). All these cases are diachronic, and it is a general fact that files deployed at different times can only support the weak CDJ relation.[7] Because confusion can always arise as information is collected across time (Millikan 1997: 517), file-stages deployed at different times—even deployments of the same dynamic file, as in the infelicitous tracking example—cannot be coreferential *de jure* in the strong sense. That is most obvious when the file undergoes fusion or fission, but that holds also for the simpler types of example, without fusion or fission.

What about files deployed at the same time—synchronous files?[8] Unless distinct points of view are brought together, as

---

[7] For discussion of a possible exception (the phenomenon of failsafe updating), see Section 5.5.

[8] A reader for Oxford University Press asked: 'If mental files are mental particulars, what does it mean to speak of "two synchronous deployments of the same file"?' By this I mean that the file that is deployed is simultaneously associated with two distinct expressions, or (in thought) with two different argument positions. It does double duty.

when indexed files come into the picture, the situation is rather neat. Two synchronous deployments are either deployments of the same file, or deployments of distinct files. Two synchronous deployments of the same file stand in the *strong* CDJ relation to each other—they are known to corefer if either refers—while deployments of distinct files can only be coreferential *de facto* (it may be that one file refers to A while the other refers to B). With diachronic deployments of files the situation is a lot messier because of the possibility of confusion (type 3), due to failure of the world to cooperate. Of course, confusion is *always* possible, but not all confusion has to be of type 3. Confusion of type 2 is compatible with strong CDJ, and that is the sort of case we encounter with synchronous files. If the subject is confused, the file she deploys fails to refer, *and fails to refer on all of its (synchronous) deployments*. No referential divergence is therefore generated when the file is deployed twice. This suggests that the shift from strong CDJ to weak CDJ can be avoided in the case of synchronous files.

3.4. *Fixing the Point of View: Strong CDJ Restored*

What I said of the Wally–Zach *interpersonal* case can be extended to the *diachronic* cases. The Wally–Zach case involves two points of view: that of Zach (the person in the CDJ state) and that of Wally. I said that if we focus on Zach's point of view we find that he associates *the same file* with the two pronouns respectively uttered by Wally and by himself. Weak CDJ characterizes the case in which different points of view are mixed, but if we fix the point of view strong CDJ is restored. The same considerations apply to the diachronic cases. In the diachronic cases, the two file-stages that are said to stand in the weak CDJ relation correspond to different temporal points of view. If we *fix* the temporal point of view and focus on, e.g., the subject after t_2 (in the infelicitous tracking example), strong CDJ is restored. Even if the subject (after t_2) thinks of the object he was perceiving before t_2, he will think of it under the confused file resting on the mistaken identity presupposition: so the two deployments of the inclusive file (in thinking of the object as it was before t_2, and in thinking of the object as it is now) corefer if either refers. (Since we assume that the identity is mistaken, both deployments fail to refer; this is a case of type 2, not type 3.)

To be sure, the subject may attempt to refer *specifically* to the object perceived before t_2 (rather than the object she is currently perceiving), if she entertains the suspicion that a substitution may have occurred. In that case, however, she will *split* the inclusive file and refer through to two distinct 'daughter files'. I describe such a case of fission in Section 5.3:

At t_1, I see a certain object and open a demonstrative file DEM$_1$ about it: 'that thing'. At t_2, the object I have been in contact with since t_1 disintegrates, but the demonstrative file persists because, as a result of taking a certain drug, I hallucinate the continued presence of the object. [...] At t_3 a doubt occurs to me and I wonder whether the object I remember seeing at the beginning of the episode (t_1) is really the same as the object that I (mistakenly) take myself to seeing at t_3. Rational doubts about identity necessarily involve two distinct mental files, and here the two files result from splitting DEM$_1$, which is replaced by a memory demonstrative (referring to the object initially seen) and a perceptual demonstrative (purporting to refer to the object currently seen).

In this example, there are, in diachrony, four different file-stages to consider. The demonstrative file opened at t_1 and maintained until t_3 (despite the disappearance of the object at t_2), is deployed both before and after t_2. Before t_2 it refers to A. Between t_2 and t_3 it fails to refer. At t_3 fission occurs and two new files come into existence: a memory file about the object initially seen, and a demonstrative file about the object the subject hallucinates. The memory file refers to A (the object the subject remembers seeing) and the demonstrative file fails to refer (because the subject is hallucinating). Let us call the four file-stages α, β, γ and δ. File α is deployed before t_2, and file β is 'the same file' deployed afterwards, in the interval between t_2 and t_3. Files γ and δ are deployed after t_3 (the time of the split). Now, what are the coreference relations between the four file-stages? The initial file α stands in the weak CDJ relation to its successor β, since β embodies a fallible presupposition of identity. File β is, with respect to α, an 'inclusive', identity-dependent file, susceptible to type 3 cases of mistaken identity. So files α and β cannot stand in the strong CDJ relation; they can only instantiate weak CDJ. Files γ and δ result from splitting β, and they are not coreferential *de jure* at all: as I have described the case, the subject suspects that they might not corefer, which is why the inclusive file β was split in the first place. However, file γ and file δ each stand in the relation of weak CDJ to file β: if the identity presupposed by β is mistaken, β fails to refer but that does not prevent γ (and, for all the subject knows, δ) from referring.

If we fix the temporal point of view, instead of looking at the coreference relations of files deployed at different times, strong CDJ is immediately restored. Between t_2 and t_3 the confused subject will deploy β *both* to think about the (hallucinated) object she takes herself to be seeing and to think about A, the object initially seen. The reason is that, after t_2, *α is no longer available to think about A*—it has been superseded by β. So instead of two deployments of distinct files standing in the weak CDJ relation, we have two deployments of the same file β. These deployments, and the singular terms associated with them, are coreferential *de jure* in the strong sense: they corefer if either refers. (Actually, they don't refer.)

These examples, as described, do not involve language, and the CDJ relations hold directly between files rather than between singular terms. But we can let the subject speak! Between t_2 and t_3 the subject might say:

(6)   That object$_\beta$ was F but it$_\beta$ is now G.

After t_3, when she starts doubting, the subject might say:

(7)   I wonder whether (that object)$_\gamma$, which was F, is (that object)$_\delta$, which is G, or whether a substitution occurred unbeknown to me.

In (6), 'that object' and 'it' are associated with the same file, namely the confused file β. So they are coreferential *de jure* in the strong sense. No diachrony is involved, even though the first clause, in the past tense, talks about the situation between t_1 and t_2, and the second clause talks about the current situation (after t_2). No diachrony is involved because the two deployments of β (in association with the demonstrative and with the pronoun) are synchronous deployments, or 'co-deployments'. In (7), however, the subject refers to the same putative object(s) by deploying two distinct files γ and δ. These files, and the terms they are associated with, are not coreferential *de jure* at all.

I conclude that synchronic deployments of the same file exhibit strong coreference *de jure*, while diachronic deployments, and the dynamic files (sequences of file-stages) they give rise to, only support weak CDJ. Weak CDJ is intransitive, while strong CDJ is transitive. Now, when we analyse an utterance or a thought, which notion of coreference *de jure* between constituents of the utterance or thought should we use? Answer: the strong one, because the files associated with distinct constituents in an utterance are *codeployed in the thought which is the output of the interpretation process*. Either it is the same file that is codeployed, and the two deployments stand in the strong CDJ relation, or it is distinct files and the coreference is, at best, *de facto*.

The only exception to that principle is the case in which distinct points of view are simultaneously at play, in the interpretation of an utterance in which one or several terms are associated with indexed files (Section 3.2). In that type of case, strong CDJ is still ruled out between the terms associated with distinct files, but the weaker form of coreference *de jure* enjoyed by diachronic deployments is now available in synchrony, via the mechanism of indexed files. That type of case, to which Pinillos has drawn our attention, is important because it reveals the intransitivity of the weak CDJ relation, but it is *not* a counterexample to the general principle I want to reassert: two terms are coreferential *de jure* (in the strong sense) if and only if they are associated with the same file.

4

Coreference De Jure and Sentence Grammar

4.1. Referential Dependency: Evans

EVANS (1980) treats anaphora as a specific form of linguistic dependency, namely *referential dependency*. One term depends upon another for its reference. Whenever that is the case, there is coreference *de jure* between the referentially dependent expression and its antecedent: one does not understand the statement unless one realizes that the two expressions corefer. Evans's notion of referential dependency is asymmetric, while coreference *de jure* is symmetric, but the relation between them is clear enough: referential dependency entails coreference *de jure* between the dependent term and its antecedent. (As we have seen, the entailment is unidirectional: there can be coreference *de jure* without referential dependency, as between two occurrences of the same name.)

Referential dependency can be intersentential, as in (1), so it is not a matter of sentence grammar:

(1)   I saw John the other day. He was wearing a blue hat.

That does not mean that sentence grammar is irrelevant. If the referentially dependent term occurs in the same sentence as its antecedent, it must obey a syntactic condition which I will call condition F: the dependent term (typically a pronoun) must not c-command its antecedent.[1] Still, referential dependency per se is not a sentence-internal phenomenon, in contrast to binding. Binding *is* a sentence-internal phenomenon, because it can *only* occur sentence-internally. It does so under strict conditions: M can bind N only if M c-commands N.[2] This condition I will refer as condition G.

Binding does not entail referential dependency, since a quantificational antecedent does not refer to anything. Yet, according to Evans (1980), it entails referential dependency *at the level of the substitution instances*: a pronoun bound by a quantificational antecedent is *eo ipso* referentially dependent upon its (singular) antecedent in all the sentences that are *substitution instances* for the quantified statement. In simpler terms: the quantificational statement is *a generalization over singular statements involving referential dependency*:

Singular instance
John loves his mother, Mark loves his mother, etc.

Quantificational generalization
(Every boy)$_i$ loves his$_i$ mother.

As I said already, quantificational binding of a pronoun is *only* possible if the pronoun stands in the right intra-sentential syntactic relation to its antecedent. If condition G is not satisfied, quantificational

---

[1] See Safir 2004: 40 and the references therein.

[2] This actually is a simplification. The right generalization has to be more complex, to accommodate examples like 'Somebody from (every city)$_i$ hates it$_i$'; but the details do not matter for my purposes. (The only thing that matters is that there *is* a syntactic constraint on quantificational binding, a constraint I refer to as 'Condition G'.)

generalization is impossible. That is arguably what happens in (2): the pronoun and its 'antecedent' do not stand in the right syntactic relation, so quantificational generalization is ruled out—it is impossible to substitute a quantifier for the referential antecedent while maintaining the relation of dependence of the pronoun on its antecedent:[3]

Singular instance

(2)   Her mother loves Jane.

Failed quantificational generalization

(2a)   *Her$_i$ mother loves (every girl)$_i$.

The fact that the pronoun and its antecedent do not stand in the right syntactic relation for binding to be possible does not prevent the pronoun in (2) from being referentially dependent upon the name, however. Condition G, necessary for binding, fails to obtain, but condition G is not necessary for referential dependency. What is necessary is condition F, and it obtains: the pronoun does not c-command its antecedent.

Indirect evidence for referential dependency is provided by the fact that, in (2), the pronoun and its antecedent are coreferential *de jure* by our tests (which is what we expect if the pronoun depends upon its antecedent). Should anyone wonder whether or not the pronoun corefers with its antecedent in (2), that would be evidence that that person has not (yet) understood the statement. This is very different from a case of mere 'intended coreference' such as (3) (adapted from Higginbotham 1985):

(3)   A. —Who is that guy?

      B. —He put on John's coat, so he must be John.

---

[3] Because of the possibility of covert movement, the c-command constraint by itself is not sufficient to rule out (2a). A better example would be the pair 'Her mother says that Jane is nice' vs *'Her$_i$ mother says that (every girl)$_i$ is nice', where covert movement is not among the options.

Speaker B intends the pronoun 'he' to corefer with 'John', but it is possible to *understand* B's utterance even though one doubts the truth of the second conjunct and therefore wonders whether the pronoun actually corefers with 'John'. In such a case there is intended coreference (and that is mutually manifest to the interlocutors), but that is not sufficient to secure coreference *de jure*, which is a stronger notion. If, following my policy in this book, we use coindexing to represent coreference *de jure*, the contrast between (2) and B's utterance in (3) can be represented as follows:

> Her_1 mother loves Jane_1
> He_1 put on John_2's coat, so he_1 must be John_2.

To make the contrast even more visible, we can construct a variant of (2) in which, as in B's utterance in (3), the pronoun and the name are coreferential *de facto* rather than *de jure*:

> Her_2 mother loves Jane_1.

Suppose the speaker points to a certain girl while uttering the pronoun 'her'. The pronoun is now used demonstratively and refers to the demonstrated girl. The statement says *of that girl* that her mother loves Jane. If the demonstrated girl turns out to be Jane herself, there is coreference *de facto* (her = Jane), but two distinct mental files are deployed, one associated with the demonstrative pronoun, the other with the name (Heim 1998: 214–15, Büring 2005: 151–9). In (2), there is a *single* mental file associated with the pronoun *and* the name.

To sum up, there are four distinct notions in Evans's system as I understand it:[4] quantificational binding of pronouns, referential

---

[4] My understanding is different from Safir's in two main respects. Like Fiengo and May (1994), I take the sort of 'dependency' revealed by the possibility of sloppy identity readings under ellipsis to be distinct from Evans's 'referential dependency', while Safir (1998) works with a unitary notion of dependency that covers both. Accordingly, Safir considers as instances of *dependency failure* cases such as (2) in which, I take it, there *is* referential dependency in Evans's sense.

dependency, coreference *de jure*, and 'intended *de facto* coreference'. Binding is a sentence-internal notion, in contrast to referential dependency. Although not a sentence-internal notion, referential dependency is subject to a strict linguistic condition when it occurs sentence-internally. Referential dependency entails coreference *de jure*, but coreference *de jure* does not obey strict linguistic conditions. There can be coreference *de jure* between two terms M and N in a sentence even if M and N do not satisfy condition F. I take this point to be implicit in Evans's paper 'Pronouns', but the discussions I have seen (e.g. by Safir 1998) tend to neglect some of the relevant distinctions and end up conflating cases such as (3), in which there is intended *de facto* coreference, and cases in which there is coreference *de jure* in the absence of condition F. What follows is an example of such a case, which shows that coreference *de jure* is not subject to the linguistic restriction Evans places on referential dependency.

4.2. *Coreference* De Jure *Without* *Grammatical Constraints*

Consider the following example, in which, because condition F does not obtain, referential dependency of the pronoun on the name is impossible:

*He loves John.

Nothing prevents the pronoun from being referentially dependent upon *another* occurrence of the name 'John', one it doesn't c-command, as in the following discourse (Evans 1985: 246):

(4)   What do you mean John loves no one? He loves John.

Let's assume that the two occurrences of the name 'John' are coreferential *de jure*. (The assumption will be scrutinized later.)

The pronoun itself is coreferential *de jure* with the first occurrence of 'John' (since it is referentially dependent on it, and referential dependency entails coreference *de jure*). It follows, by transitivity, that the pronoun is also coreferential *de jure* with the second occurrence of the name 'John'.[5] Conclusion: a pronoun may be coreferential *de jure* with a name in a sentence even if referential dependency on that name is precluded by the failure of condition F.

In assuming that the two occurrences of 'John' in utterance (4) are coreferential *de jure*, I have in effect accepted the following as the correct representation of (4):

(5)   What do you mean John$_1$ loves no one? He$_1$ loves John$_1$.

But one may deny what I have assumed, and put forward the following, alternative representation:

(6)   What do you mean John$_1$ loves no one? He$_1$ loves John$_2$.

This representation, with the two occurrences of the name 'John' contra-indexed, makes (4) similar to (3B), i.e. B's utterance in (3). In the first conjunct of (3B) the speaker speaks as if 'he' and 'John' were two distinct persons ('he put on John's coat'). In the second conjunct she says that they are the same ('he must be John') but expresses the identity by deploying two distinct files (one for the man they are looking at, the other for John) and, as it were, linking them. As Safir puts it (1998: 141) identity statements 'assert that two terms not known to be covalued do indeed have the same value'. Because the identity is not presupposed (but asserted) it is possible to understand the statement even if one does not believe the identity that is asserted. That shows that the coreference is only

---

[5] As we have seen, there are two notions of coreference *de jure*: one is transitive and the other is not. Here I am appealing to the transitive notion ('strong' coreference *de jure*).

de facto, even in the second clause (the identity statement). So the proper representation of the example is, as I said already:

He$_1$ put on John$_2$'s coat, so he$_1$ must be John$_2$.

Again, the indices correspond to mental files in the minds of the discourse protagonists (Heim 1998 speaks of 'guises'). If two terms are contra-indexed, that means that they are associated with distinct mental files, as in 'He must be John'. In such a case, it is still possible for the two terms to be coreferential, and intended as such. In the absence of coindexing, there may still be covaluation, but covaluation will take place only if the two distinct mental files associated with two terms that are not coindexed happen to be mental files about the same thing.

Can we treat utterance (4) similarly and deny that coreference *de jure* obtains between the two occurrences of the name? Can we maintain (6) as a representation of utterance (4)? If we use the standard test, it will be clear that we cannot. Someone who does not understand that the person John is said to love is John himself has not understood utterance (4). One can understand (3) even if one does not believe that the guy one is looking at is John; but one cannot understand (4) if one does not believe that the person John is said to love is John himself. This establishes that the two occurrences of 'John' in utterance (4) are coreferential *de jure*, not *de facto*.

It is true that there is something special about (4). John's self-love is described as if it was love for someone else. That is due to two factors. First, there is the parallelism established between 'loves no one' and 'loves John'.[6] In 'John loves no one', the domain of quantification is implicitly restricted to persons other than the subject. The parallelism suggests that the person John is said to love, namely John, falls within the domain of quantification. John's loving himself is therefore treated as an instance of John's loving someone other than himself. This pragmatic effect is reinforced by

---

[6] On the effect of parallelism on interpretation, see Kehler (2002).

the second factor: John's self-love is not described in the most straightforward way, as it would be if the speaker had said 'John loves himself'. As many people have noted, the expression of coreference *de jure* in language is regulated by a preference for using the 'most dependent' expression available in the syntactic context (Reinhart 1983, Safir 1998, 2004). When the most dependent expression is not used, as in (4), this generates what Safir calls an 'expectation of non-covaluation'. The lovee is expected to be different from the lover. Such an expectation can lead the interpreter to understand the utterance as expressing coreference *de facto* rather than *de jure*. (That is arguably what happens in (3).) But it is also possible for the interpreter to *overcome* the expectation, if the context is suitable. That is what happens in (4), and in all the examples Evans provides for showing that expectations of non-covaluation can be overcome in context. Although, in (4), the expectation that the lover and the lovee are distinct persons is eventually overcome, the pragmatic effect generated by the two factors is still felt and colours the discourse with an ironic overtone. What is ironical is the fact that B presents John's self-love as an instance of the sort of love John is said by A to lack (love for others), while it actually confirms that John is interested in himself and not in others.

So I maintain that the two occurrences of the name 'John' in utterance (4) are coreferential *de jure*.[7] Since coreference *de jure* also

---

[7] The *de jure* coreferential interpretation of (4) represented in (5) violates the standard conditions of Binding Theory. On Reinhart's approach, however, these conditions do not apply directly to a logical form such as (5); they primarily apply to the logical form's *binding alternatives* (since binding is syntactically represented while coreference *de jure* is not). The Binding Conditions apply to a logical form such as (5) only indirectly, via 'interface rules' (Reinhart 2006): (5) is ruled out if it is *semantically undistinguishable* from syntactically illicit binding alternatives. In our example, the ironic effect induced by using the name instead of the reflexive in the second clause apparently counts as a semantic difference sufficient to make the sentence acceptable on its *de jure* coreferential interpretation. If this is right, then perhaps it is not just 'structured meanings' that matter when semantic indistinguishability requires more than propositional identity (Heim 1998). (On semantic indistinguishability and its role in interface rules, see Roelofsen 2010.)

holds between the pronoun and the first occurrence of the name, it follows by transitivity that it holds between the pronoun and the second occurrence of the name, even though their syntactic relation does not satisfy condition F. This establishes that coreference *de jure* is not grammatically constrained, as referential dependency is. To be sure, there is a general *preference* for expressing coreference *de jure* using the most dependent form available in the syntactic context, but such a preference, which may be overcome, is very different from the strict linguistic rules which govern sentence-internal referential dependency (condition F) or binding (condition G).

The fact that coreference *de jure* is unconstrained, from a grammatical point of view, invites a 'pragmatic' approach according to which it is not a grammatical relation at all. Such a view, forcefully argued for by Reinhart (1983), has become the mainstream position nowadays (see e.g. Safir 1998, Neale 2005, Reuland 2011). Only a minority of linguists treat coreference *de jure* as 'grammatically determined coreference', as Fiengo and May (1994) put it. I will consider that debate in Section 4.4.

4.3. *Grammatical Dependency vs 'Accidental Coreference'*

Even though there are already four distinct notions in Evans's system, a fifth one, unacknowledged by Evans, needs to be taken on board: what Fiengo and May (1994) refer to as 'syntactic dependency', and which I will call 'grammatical dependency'. Grammatical dependency is revealed by the possibility of a sloppy reading of the pronoun under ellipsis.

Consider (7):

(7)   John likes his new teacher, and his parents do too.

Presumably, the second clause means that John's parents too like John's new teacher. That is the 'strict' reading. But there is another reading of (7) on which the second clause means that John's parents too like *their* new teacher. That is the 'sloppy' reading. It is standard to consider that the availability of the two readings discloses a hidden ambiguity in the first clause.[8] In 'John likes his new teacher', the pronoun 'his' may or may not be *grammatically dependent* on its antecedent. Grammatical dependency in the first clause is what explains the sloppy reading in the second clause.

If the pronoun is grammatically dependent, it is not directly interpretable but is linked to its antecedent and only gets interpreted through the latter. This, Fiengo and May argue, is different from Evans's referential dependency. When a pronoun is *referentially* dependent upon its singular antecedent, it gets its value from a contextual assignment, under the constraint that that value must be the same as the value assigned to the antecedent. (For Fiengo and May, that constraint is a consequence of 'syntactic identity', where syntactic identity is what is expressed by coindexing the pronoun and its antecedent.) When a pronoun is *grammatically* dependent upon its antecedent, however, it does not receive a referential value directly. As Fiengo and May put it, 'there is a difference between reference being given once for a structure and reference being given many times over' (Fiengo and May 1994: 51). That difference persists even when (because of coindexing) the 'reference being given many times over' is constrained to be *the same reference each time* (coreference *de jure*).

In Fiengo's and May's system there are two types of indices associated with occurrences of singular terms: an α or β index, which marks the fact that the term is grammatically dependent (β) or independent (α), and a numerical index ($1, 2, \ldots n$) whose role is to mark coreference *de jure* through coindexing (or the lack of

---

[8] The ambiguity is hidden because the two readings of the first clause (with or without grammatical dependency) are truth-conditionally equivalent.

coreference *de jure* through contra-indexing). Coreference *de jure* holds whenever two singular terms are coindexed, *whether or not there is (additionally) a relation of grammatical dependency between them*. As Fiengo and May explain:

Two sub-cases are subsumed under co-indexing: independence—co-indexing among α-occurrences—and dependence—co-indexing between an α-occurrence and β-occurrences.[9] Both of these circumstances hold for expressions that are grammatically determined to be co-valued [= coreferential *de jure*], since this is a matter solely of co-indexing. [...] The coreference that arises among [α-]occurrences is as much grammatically determined, in virtue of co-indexing, as the coreference that arises with β-occurrences. Thus, this circumstance is not comparable to the one that arises when there is no referential dependency, in Evans' sense.   (Fiengo and May 1994: 82–4)

By and large, the syntactic configuration which makes binding possible also makes sloppy readings possible. That generalization, initially put forward by Lasnik (1976), is not without exceptions, but it has seemed robust enough to motivate the attempt, by Reinhart and her followers, to *reduce* grammatical dependency to binding (Reinhart 1983). According to Reinhart, sloppy readings under ellipsis are possible when the pronoun in the overt clause is *bound by an abstraction operator*. The two readings of 'John loves his mother', revealed through the addition of a conjoined elliptical clause ('and Peter does too'), can be represented as follows:

Strict reading

John$_1$ loves his$_1$ mother, and Peter$_2$ ~~loves his$_1$ mother~~ too (i.e. Peter too loves John's mother).

Sloppy reading

John$_1$ (λx loves x's mother), and Peter$_2$ ~~($\lambda x.\ x$ loves x's mother)~~ too (i.e. Peter too loves his own mother).

---

[9] Names like 'John' can only be independent, according to Fiengo and May: their indices are always of the independent type (α-occurrences).

Fiengo and May acknowledge the close connection between grammatical dependency and binding but they strive to keep the two notions distinct. Grammatical dependency is a linear relation, they say, while binding is a hierarchical one (Fiengo and May 1994: 81–2). Rather than reducing dependency to binding, they analyse pronominal binding as resting on grammatical dependency: a pronoun is bound by a quantifier just in case it is *grammatically dependent upon a variable bound by a quantifier*, as in (8):

(8)   Everyone$_1$ [e$_{\alpha 1}$ saw his$_{\beta 1}$ mother];

'The valuation of a pronoun bearing a β-occurrence that is co-indexed with a variable will proceed in terms of that variable' (Fiengo and May 1994: 75), so the pronoun winds up bound by the quantifier.

As far as we are concerned, the exact relation between grammatical dependency and binding does not matter. What matters is that grammatical dependency and binding are both sentence-internal relations. That is not the case for Evans's referential dependency, let alone for coreference *de jure*. This has led many authors to the view that *coindexing between grammatically independent occurrences* reflects the speaker's *communicative intentions*, rather than any properly grammatical feature of the sentence. Dependency / binding is grammatical, on that view, but coreference *de jure* is not. Thus Lasnik, Reinhart, and their followers put cases of coindexing between independent occurrences in the same basket as cases of intended *de facto* coreference. They speak of 'accidental coreference' for all these cases. The following quote (from Schlenker) is typical:

In a sentence such as *His mother likes John*, where *his* denotes John, we [. . .] follow Reinhart (1983) in claiming that there is no formal connection between the free pronoun *his* and what is intuitively its antecedent, namely *John*; accordingly, we treat *his* as being demonstrative in our sense (=deictic).   (Schlenker 2005: 11)

Of course, the pronoun 'her' in 'her mother loves Jane' can be anaphoric (on 'Jane') rather than deictic. (Those are two clearly distinct readings.) But the theory put forward by Reinhart treats these two uses as relevantly similar: since the pronoun is not grammatically dependent (bound), it is free and valued through a contextual assignment. This is what Schlenker means when he writes that the pronoun is 'demonstrative' or 'deictic' in (2).

Another, often discussed example similar to (2) is:

(9)   Pictures of John's father belong to him,

where 'him' may be anaphoric on, hence coreferential *de jure* with, the name 'John' in the embedded description 'John's father'. Since the name does not c-command the pronoun, the pronoun is grammatically independent, hence counts as 'free' in Reinhart's framework. In contrast to Fiengo and May, who treat coreference *de jure* relations between singular terms as grammatically marked through numerical coindexing ('Pictures of John$_1$'s father belong to him$_1$'), Reinhart and her followers treats them as linguistically *unmarked*: coreference *de jure* is entirely a matter of pragmatics, and from a grammatical point of view there is no significant difference between true deictic uses and unbound anaphoric uses.

Reuland summarizes the debate as follows:

In Reinhart's approach, [...] it is entirely proper to represent the sentence (9) as in (9a) without indices. The syntactic structure does not prescribe whether (9a) is assigned the interpretation (9b), (9c), and so on.

(9a)   Pictures of John's father belong to him
(9b)   Pictures of John's father belong to him & him = John
(9c)   Pictures of John's father belong to him & him = Peter

That is, assigning *him* and *John* the same individual as their value has the same status in the theory as assigning *him* any other male individual as a value. What value is actually assigned is fully determined by the interpretive component. In Reinhart's approach the interpretation represented by (9b) typically instantiates what has been called 'accidental coreference'. In a Fiengo-and-May type approach, 'accidental coreference' is limited to cases like ['He must be John'] where to the relevant parties involved it is not known whether *John* is actually identical to *he*'. (Reuland 2011: 54)

As we are about to see, there are two distinct issues here, which are worth disentangling. Disentangling them reveals the possibility of a *hybrid view*, combining aspects of Reinhart's position and aspects of Fiengo and May's.

4.4. *Syntax, Pragmatics, and 'Logical Form'*

The *first issue* in the debate summarized by Reuland is this: Do cases of *de jure* coreference such as (2) and cases of intended *de facto* coreference such as (3B) belong to the same natural kind (so-called 'accidental coreference'), as Reinhart and her followers sometimes suggest? Or are they different beasts, as Evans claimed and Fiengo and May maintain? On this issue I unambiguously side with Evans and Fiengo and May.

The major problem I see with the ideology of 'accidental coreference' is that, focused on one contrast (between bound and free variables, or dependent and independent occurrences), it ignores another—the difference between coreference *de facto* and *de jure*. But the *de jure*/*de facto* contrast is no less important than the other one. Cases like (3B) deserve the label 'accidental coreference' because two distinct files are involved, which turn out to be about the same entity. In a case like (2), however, there is a single file, and this guarantees that the two occurrences associated with that unique file corefer. Being guaranteed, the coreference at stake is in no way 'accidental', even if it is not linguistically marked (i.e. guaranteed *by the grammar*).

Stephen Neale is one of the philosophers who forcefully argue in favour of the view that there are only two things: binding and 'mere' coreference. He proposes to 'dispens[e] with *de jure* co-reference altogether in a final theory of anaphora' (Neale 2005: 247). As he puts it:

Every pronoun seemingly anaphoric on a name *a* (or any other referring expression) is either (i) bound by *a* (in the usual semantic sense) or else (ii) an occurrence of an indexical that is merely coreferential with *a*. (Neale 2005: 205)

Mere coreference is, according to him, a case of *independent* reference to an object which has been mentioned before. It is not dependent reference. The only sort of dependent reference, for Neale, is binding.

Neale provides what looks like an argument for positing a simple distinction between binding and mere coreference, rather than a more complex picture with three distinct things (*de facto* coreference, coreference *de jure*, and binding). According to this argument, alleged cases of 'referential dependency without binding' fall into the same category as ordinary cases of indexical reference to some object given or made salient in the context of utterance. This category contrasts with the cases in which the interpretation of the pronoun is secured *as soon as the dependency relation between the pronoun and its antecedent is identified*. When there is no grammatical dependency, the interpretation of the pronoun requires extra pragmatic work, Neale says. The reference of the pronoun has to be *independently identified*. That characteristic feature of free pronouns is common to ordinary indexical reference and to alleged cases of referential dependency without binding:

Identifying whether [in 'John loves his mother'] A is using /his/ in the bound or in the indexical way *is* a pragmatic matter: although B's knowledge of word meaning and syntax tell B that A must be using /his/ in either the bound or indexical way, it does not provide B with enough information to establish *which one A intends* on any particular occasion. At the same time, *if A* is using /his/ in the bound way, then the pronoun's interpretation is *fixed relative to that use*: if B happens to know that *A* is using /his/ in the bound way—suppose, for the sake of argument, that *A* reveals this to *B*—there is no *further* pragmatic work for *B* to do with respect to /his/: its interpretation is now secured. By contrast, *if A* is avowedly using /his/ in the indexical way, there is still some pragmatic work for *B* to do: *B* needs to establish whether *A* is using /his/ to refer to, say, John, or Paul, or George or Ringo. (Neale 2005: 250)

Neale suggests that in alleged cases of referential dependency, the interpretation of the pronoun is completed at the same 'late' pragmatic level as in cases of independent indexical reference. But I deny that. The extra pragmatic work of identifying the reference in context is only required when there is no dependency, *whether grammatical or referential*. Neale's argument begs the question against Evans, by assuming that the only kind of dependency there is is grammatical dependency (binding). What Neale says about the bound case (that no pragmatic work needs to be done after the dependent use of the pronoun has been identified) can be said *also* about referential dependency. When a pronoun is referentially dependent upon its antecedent in Evans's sense (thereby securing coreference *de jure*), the only interpretive work that has to be done is to identify the dependency relation between the pronoun and its antecedent. Once that is done, no *further* pragmatic task awaits the interpreter: the reference of the pronoun has got to be that of its antecedent, so it does not have to be 'independently identified'. This is a point Evans makes when he says that anaphora is a matter of rule, and that the only pragmatic task facing the interpreter consists in identifying the relation of referential dependence which holds, in virtue of the speaker's intentions, between the pronoun and its antecedent.

The *second issue* in the debate summarized by Reuland concerns the division of labour between grammar and pragmatics:

In a Fiengo-and-May approach, the bulk of the work is done in the syntax by indexing, and only a marginal part of it is left to an interpretive component. In a Reinhart type of approach the work is rather equally divided over the interpretive component and the computational system (syntax and logical form governing binding relations), leading to a modular approach to binding in which indices are not part of the syntactic structure. (Reuland 2011: 54–5)

'Syntax and logical form' yield what Reuland refers to as *logical syntax*, namely:

a formal representation of the output of the computational system with the degree of detail required by the inference system (and independently justified because of the requirements of the inference system). Essentially, it is syntax with an extended vocabulary.   (Reuland 2011: 34)

Does coindexing belong to that level, or does it not? That is the question. To answer it, we must start by clarifying the notion of 'logical form' which has just been introduced in connection with the requirements of the 'inference system'.

As Reuland's words suggest, there are 'details' that the inference system must see to do its work. Among them, undoubtedly, we find relations of coreference *de jure* between singular terms. As Kaplan emphasizes, the indexing difference between (10) and (11) is essential from the point of view of logic—(10) is a logical truth (an instance of the Law of Double Negation) while (11) isn't, even if the demonstration associated with the pronoun in the second clause of (11) manifestly targets the same individual as the demonstrative 'this student' in the first clause:

(10)   This student$_1$ won't pass so it is not the case that he$_1$ will pass.

(11)   This student$_1$ won't pass so it is not the case that he$_2$ will pass.

Coindexing carries information regarding the very structure of the conceptual representation (the thought) associated with an utterance: it correspond to the fact that the same mental file is deployed twice, in such a way that coreference is guaranteed (assuming the terms actually refer). There is no reason why that piece of structural information should be deemed less important to the inferential system than the determination of the scope of quantifiers or the choice between a collective and a distributive interpretation. Coindexing is undoubtedly an aspect of logical form, in the traditional (philosophical) sense of that phrase.

Still, coreference *de jure* need not be established *in the syntax*. It needs to be fixed at some level of 'logical form', but that need not be the level that is the direct output of the computational system—it may be an intermediate level generated by the interpretive system in processing the utterance. Such a level is what, in *Truth-Conditional Pragmatics* (2010), I call *enriched logical form* and which Roelofsen (2010) calls *extended logical form*. On this picture, intermediate between Reinhart's and Fiengo and May's, the logical form of an utterance is partly *underdetermined by sentence grammar*. Essential though they are from a logical point of view, coindexing relations are left out: grammatical dependency is linguistically encoded, but referential dependency isn't.

One might think that referential dependency is *lexically* encoded. It is tempting to construe lexical anaphors, e.g. reflexives in English, as encoding (and thereby enforcing) referential dependency. In the same spirit, Kaplan has put forward the view that demonstratives carry a lexical feature which *precludes* referential dependency. According to him:

In natural language every new syntactic occurrence of a true demonstrative requires not just a referent-determining intention, but a *new* referent-determining intention. When two syntactic occurrences of a demonstrative appear to be linked to a single intention, at least one must be anaphoric. When we wish to refer to the referent of an earlier demonstrative, we do not repeat the demonstrative, we use an anaphoric pronoun, 'He [pointing] won't pass unless he [anaphoric pronoun] studies.' The fact that demonstrative and anaphoric pronouns are

homonyms may have led to confusion on this point. The case is clearer
when the demonstrative is not homonymous with the anaphoric pronoun. Contrast, 'This student [pointing] won't pass unless he [anaphoric
pronoun] studies' with 'This student [pointing] won't pass unless this
student [pointing a second time at what is believed to be the same person]
studies.' The awkwardness of the second, shows that the way to secure a
second reference to the referent of a demonstrative, is to use an anaphor.
(Kaplan 1989b: 588–9)

The difference Kaplan is talking about is that between:

> (12) This student$_1$ won't pass unless he$_1$ studies (demonstra-
> tive + anaphoric pronoun),

and

> (13) This student$_1$ wont pass unless this student$_2$ studies
> (demonstrative + contra-indexed demonstrative).

What is ruled out by the lexical semantics of demonstratives,
according to Kaplan, is:

> (14) *This student$_1$ wont pass unless this student$_1$ studies
> (demonstrative + coindexed demonstrative).

Distinct syntactic occurrences of a demonstrative cannot be coindexed because 'the directing intention is the element that differen-
tiates the "meaning" of one syntactic occurrence of a demonstrative
from another, creating the potential for distinct referents' (Kaplan
1989b: 588). As a result, just as the Law of Double Negation cannot
be validly expressed using demonstratives, an identity statement can
never be 'trivial' or 'uninformative' if it is expressed using demonstratives, as in (15):

> (15) That is that.

If Kaplan is right about demonstratives, even if the two occurrences of 'that' corefer, (15) is not an instance of the Law of
Identity, any more than (11) is an instance of the Law of Double

Negation. Given the constraint of contra-indexing for demonstratives, the logical form of (15) is:

(16)   That$_1$ is that$_2$.

On Kaplan's view as I understand it, demonstratives are −anaphoric, reflexive pronouns are (presumably) +anaphoric, and non-reflexive pronouns are ambiguous between a +anaphoric and a −anaphoric reading. Rather than talk of 'homonymy', as Kaplan does, one might say that non-reflexive pronouns are underspecified in the relevant dimension (+/−anaphoric). If this view is correct, referential dependency has some linguistic reality; it seems that it corresponds to a linguistic feature with two polar values.

But it is far from obvious that this view is correct. First, reflexives may be thought to encode *grammatical dependency* rather than *referential dependency*. In 'John loves himself', the VP 'loves himself' arguably denotes the property $\lambda x.x$ *loves x*, in such a way that the object of 'love' is grammatically dependent upon its subject (Salmon 1986, 1992, Büring 2005: 43–4). To be sure, grammatical dependency entails referential dependency when the antecedent of the reflexive pronoun is referential, as in this case, but the point remains: encoding grammatical dependency is not the same thing as encoding referential dependency. As for demonstratives, the sentence which Kaplan discusses, 'This student won't pass unless this student studies', does generate an 'expectation of non-covaluation' (we expect there to be two distinct students), but, as we have seen, such expectations can be explained as a (defeasible) effect of competition (Reinhart 1983, Safir 1998, 2004). This is similar to 'John believes that John will come', which through competition with 'John believes that he will come' gives rise to an expectation of non-covaluation, yielding the reading 'John$_1$ believes that John$_2$ will come'. However, that does not mean that two successive occurrences of 'John' *cannot* be coreferential *de jure*. Expectations of non-covaluation can be overcome. In the case of demonstratives, it is not too difficult to find counterexamples to

Kaplan's thesis, i.e. repeated occurrences of demonstratives that *are* coreferential *de jure* because the expectation of non-covaluation is suspended in the context at hand. The following sentence (of the sort Evans 1980 and Heim 1998 put in the mouth of a logic teacher) is a case in point:

(17)   If *everyone* hates (a certain man)$_1$, then (that man himself)$_1$ must hate (that man)$_1$.

I conclude that we *can* side with Evans and Fiengo and May, and draw a sharp distinction between coreference *de jure* and intended (*de facto*) coreference, even if, persuaded by Reinhart, we take coreference *de jure* to be a property of the conceptual representations we associate with sentences in the course of interpreting them, rather than a grammatical property of the sentences themselves. The two issues I have disentangled turn out to be orthogonal. A follower of Reinhart does not have to buy the ideology of 'accidental coreference' and can do justice to the fundamental distinction between coreference *de facto* and *de jure*. Indeed Reinhart herself and the semanticists inspired by her work have reintroduced coreference *de jure* in one form or another, and have attempted to make room for it in the theory. Heim (1998) invokes a notion of 'codetermination' which covers binding and coreference *de jure*, and reformulates Condition B of Binding Theory in terms of it (thus departing from Reinhart's insight that, contrary to binding, coreference is not syntactically represented). Büring maintains Reinhart's insight and defines coreference *de jure* (which he calls 'presupposed coreference') as coreference in all the worlds compatible with the information state of the context (Büring 2005: 154). Building on Heim's and Büring's work, Reinhart (2006) and Roelofsen (2010) account for Condition B effects and their exceptions by appealing to 'interface strategies' which forbid *de jure* coreferential interpretations if there are syntactically illicit binding alternatives with the same semantic import. In this framework, although presupposed coreference interacts with the syntax through interface strategies, it is not syntactically represented (in contrast to binding). *De jure* coreference is only represented at the level of 'extended logical form', 'which include[s] a specification of how the referential pronouns occurring in the logical form are supposed to be resolved' (Roelofsen 2010: 134). Extended logical forms correspond to *interpretations*, and that is arguably the level where coreference *de jure* belongs.

5
Cognitive Dynamics

5.1. The Problem

THE following tenets are essential to the mental file framework. They correspond to various roles which Frege assigned to 'senses', and which mental files arguably play.

- Mental files determine the reference of linguistic expressions: an expression refers to what the mental file associated with it refers to (at the time of tokening). The file itself refers via the acquaintance relations, or 'ER relations', it is based on. (ER relations are *epistemically rewarding* relations, i.e. relations to entities which make information flow possible between the subject and these entities.)

- Mental files account for cognitive significance. Frege's Constraint states that if a rational subject can believe of a given object both that it is F and that it is not F (as happens in so-called 'Frege cases'), then the subject thinks of that object under distinct modes of presentation. Now the subject's having distinct mental files about a given object is necessary and arguably sufficient to generate the possibility of Frege cases. This suggests that the files themselves, *qua* mental particulars, are what play the role of mode of presentation.

- Mental files enable coreference *de jure*. If two token singular terms M and N are associated with the same file, it is presupposed that they corefer (if they refer at all) and Trading on Identity (TI) becomes valid: one can move from 'M is *F*' and 'N is *G*' directly to 'there is an *x* which is *F* and *G*', without needing to invoke an identity premiss.

Onofri (2015) objects that mental files can't simultaneously play the FC role (satisfying Frege's Constraint) and the TI role (enabling coreference *de jure*). To play the first role, they must be fine-grained rather than coarse-grained. Fine-grainedness is characterized as follows: the more information channels a given file rests on, the less fine-grained it is. Fine-grained files (e.g. demonstrative files or memory files) are based on specific ER relations, so they are fine-grained. We need fine-grained files to play the FC role because the subject can always wonder whether, e.g., the object he sees is the object he encountered in the past and remembers. In such a case there has to be two distinct modes of presentation (by Frege's Constraint). Now to play the second role (the TI role), files must be coarse-grained, given that cross-modal and cross-temporal integration of information licenses TI. For example, if I remember that a certain object was *F* and, upon encountering it again, notice that it is *G*, I can infer: something that was *F* is now *G*. This is TI, yet the mental file deployed in the first premiss (to the effect that the remembered object was *F*) is a memory file, while the mental file deployed in the second premiss (to the effect that the seen object is *G*) is a perceptual file. These files are distinct types of file, and we can easily imagine Frege cases involving them. Or think of a case in which I see and touch a certain glass: if cross-modal integration of information occurs as it should, I will trade upon identity and infer, from 'that (seen) glass is yellow' and 'that (touched) glass is cold', that the glass is yellow and cold; but again, one can easily imagine Frege cases in which distinct files are deployed, one for each modality, without the identity being presupposed. The subject might wonder whether the yellow glass he sees is the cold glass he touches. So Frege's Constraint dictates that there be two distinct modes of presentation, while the subject's trading on identity shows that, for him, there is only one file, which integrates visual and tactile information.

So: one file, or two files? It seems that two (fine-grained) files are needed to the FC role, while a single, coarse-grained file is required to account for TI. The suggestion that a single entity accounts for both FC and TI is therefore dubious and the whole framework threatens to collapse. That is Onofri's argument against mental files.

Ninan (2015) comes to a similar conclusion, based on a different type of example:

Suppose that, at time t_1, I look at my watch and think to myself, *It's 1:00pm now*. Later (at t_2) I come to think, *Actually, it wasn't 1:00pm then; I forgot to change my watch after the flight*. Intuitively, I changed my mind between t_1 and t_2 about whether it was 1:00pm at the time in question. But my initial thought employs a *now*-file μ_1, while my later thought employs a *then*-file μ_2. According to Recanati, μ_1 and μ_2 are distinct files or modes of presentation. But then why should this count as a change of mind? Normally, if I ascribe a property to an object o while thinking of it under mode of presentation m_1 and then later ascribe an incompatible property to o while thinking of it under a distinct mode of presentation m_2, I do not thereby count as changing my mind. For example: I might think in the morning that Phosphorus is bright, but then think in the evening that Hesperus is not bright. If I am employing two distinct modes of presentation on these two occasions, this does not count as a change of mind. The reason for this seems to be that the two contents in question are not incompatible in the appropriate sense.   (Ninan 2015: 370)

The subject changes her mind only if she thinks of the object under the same mode of presentation throughout; otherwise there is no conflict, hence no change of mind has to be posited. But if the mode of presentation is the same, we can no longer equate modes of presentation with files *and* maintain that files are based on fine-grained ER relations to the object of thought; for in this case as in the others, the ER relation changes while the mode of presentation remains one and the same.

As Onofri and Ninan acknowledge, this problem is not new. It traces back to Evans's discussion of cognitive dynamics (and his introduction of 'dynamic Fregean senses') in 'Understanding Demonstratives' and *The Varieties of Reference*.[1] I devote a chapter to the problem in *Mental Files*, and I offer the following solution. A file can be *converted into* another one, to adjust to a contextual change which brings about a change in the subject's ER relations to the reference. In particular, a file may be converted into a distinct, more inclusive file based on more ER relations than the initial file ('incremental conversion'). Through incremental conversion, files grow new information links. Trading on identity across deployment of distinct ER relations is made possible by the *composite* nature of the inclusive file which is the output of incremental conversion. So in cross-temporal or cross-modal cases, a single file is used in the train of thought, and that file, in contrast to the initial, pre-conversion file, is based on *several* ER relations.[2]

I stand by my solution, but it has obviously failed to convince Onofri and Ninan. What follows is my defence of it, focused on the worries they expressed.

5.2. *Allegedly Diachronic Inferences*

Onofri thinks my solution does not work, for the revised theory faces a dilemma. Is the post-conversion file (the *inclusive file*) the same file as the pre-conversion file (the *initial file*)? If the answer is

---

[1] Evans's discussion of cognitive dynamics itself traces back to Kaplan (1989a: 537–8); see also Perry 1980a for an early discussion of the phenomenon. Later contributions to the topic include Campbell 1994, Dokic 1996, Perry 1997, Branquiñho 1999 and 2008, Prosser 2005 and forthcoming, and Dickie and Rattan 2010.

[2] Kamp (2015) emphasizes that what he calls an 'internally anchored entity representation' (a mental file) is often associated with multiple 'internal anchors' (where the internal anchors are the presupposed ER relations on which the files are based).

positive, files become coarse-grained and cannot play the FC role. If the answer is negative, the mental file account of coreference *de jure* is made redundant. What makes two token singular terms coreferential *de jure* is no longer the fact that they are associated with the same file, but the fact that the (distinct) files they are respectively associated with are related through the mechanism of conversion. It is the mechanics of conversion that does all the work. As Onofri puts it:

On this account, what is it that really explains the rationality of trading on identity? Clearly, not that the same file is involved in the inference! On the contrary, the correct explanation will now be as follows: A has produced a distinct file B through conversion, and this makes it the case that the inference is rational (perhaps together with other factors). For our purposes, it doesn't matter whether this explanation is correct. What matters is that all the explanatory work is done by the mechanism relating the files, rather than their alleged sameness. It would now be unnecessary to include the assumption 'A and B are the same file' in a complete explanation of trading on identity: file sameness has become explanatorily useless.   (Onofri 2015: 387–8)

Onofri concludes that my account 'faces the following dilemma: either the files involved in trading-on-identity inferences are literally the same, in which case files are not modes of presentation; or they are distinct but related through cognitive mechanisms like conversion, in which case the appeal to file sameness plays no role in explaining rational inferences' (Onofri 2015: 388).

But I think the objection rests on a confusion. In TI the *de jure* coreferential occurrences correspond to deployments of *the same file*, namely the inclusive file (post-conversion). So TI is still accounted in Fregean fashion, by appealing to sameness of sense (or sameness of file). This is compatible with the fact that the single file which is deployed twice in the TI train of thought is an inclusive file resulting from the conversion of an initial file, and therefore distinct from that initial file. So I maintain that the pre- and post-conversion files are *distinct* files, but that does not entail the unwelcome consequence advertised by Onofri: that 'appealing to sameness of file/mode of presentation now becomes explanatorily useless in accounting for trading on identity' (Onofri 2015: 387). The files which must be 'the same file' to preserve the account of TI in terms of file identity are *the files associated with the two token singular terms* in the TI train of thought. The terms are coreferential *de jure* because they are associated with the same file. That file is an inclusive file resulting from the conversion of an initial file, and therefore distinct from that initial file. I conclude that the distinctness of the pre- and post-conversion files does not make the appeal to file identity redundant in my account of TI.

The source of Onofri's confusion is the assumption that the pre- and post-conversion files *are* the files respectively associated with the (*de jure* coreferential) token singular terms in cross-modal or cross-temporal TI-licensing trains of thought. If this were true, Onofri's objection would go through. But I reject the assumption: I deny that the initial file *is* deployed in cross-modal or cross-temporal TI. The illusion that it is stems from the diachronic nature of the reasoning in the sort of example Onofri focuses on.

Consider the following case, similar to Onofri's own Jack/John example (Onofri 2015: 391). Remembering a certain object from a past encounter, and remembering it as *F*, I think: '*that thing* was *F*'. Then I look around, recognize the object in question in the vicinity, see that it is G (rather than *F*) and think: '*it* is G now'. Onofri would say that the first premiss involves a deployment of a pure memory file (the initial file: a 'memory demonstrative'), while the second premiss involves a deployment of the inclusive file (a 'recognitional demonstrative', resting on memory *and* perception). On that way of understanding the example, the two token singular terms are coreferential *de jure* (TI is licensed), yet they are associated with distinct files, namely the initial file and the inclusive file it converts into when the subject recognizes the object. So if we accept that there are such examples, Onofri's objection goes through.

But I deny the legitimacy of that 'diachronic' understanding of the TI train of thought.[3] For logic purposes, a train of reasoning has to be construed as synchronic (Kaplan 1989b: 584–85). Of course, we are free to stipulate that the subject had the initial thought, '*that thing* was F', at time t_1, before perceiving and recognizing the remembered object, and only later—at t_2—thought '*it* is G now'. But in this case I hold that the train of reasoning *occurring at* t_2 involves two premisses: one is the overt premiss 'it is G now', where 'it' is associated with the inclusive file, and the other one is what the subject has *retained* of the initial thought. What the subject has retained is not the initial thought itself, but a variant that *results from updating the initial thought (the thought held at* t_1*) through conversion of the initial file into the inclusive file.* Updating here is *necessary* to retention. The initial file is no longer available at t_2, so the thought in which it occurs (the thought held at t_1) cannot be directly recruited into the train of thought that takes place at t_2. At t_2, after recognition, the initial file has been converted into the inclusive file, so only the inclusive file remains and can feature in the ongoing train of thought.

If we make the associated files explicit by adding subscripts to the singular terms, we get the following representation of the TI train of thought in the example I have just discussed:

t_1:	that$_{\text{memory}}$ was F	(initial thought, featuring the pure
	$\downarrow$ *conversion*	memory file)
t_2:	**that$_{\text{memory + perception}}$ was F**	(updated thought, featuring the inclusive file based on memory *and* perception)
	that$_{\text{memory + perception}}$ is now G	(new thought, featuring the same file)

Something that was F is now G   (TI, licensed by sameness of file)

---

[3] As M. Murez pointed out to me, the position I defend in this chapter is similar to so-called 'time-slice epistemology' (Moss 2015), i.e. the view that 'the locus of rationality is the time-slice rather than the temporally extended agent' (Hedden 2015a: 449). See Hedden 2015b for a book-length defence of the view.

The initial thought, formed at t_1, must be updated in order to serve as a premiss in the reasoning taking place at t_2. Updating proceeds through conversion of the constituent file. Once conversion has taken place, the train of thought involves two deployments of the same file (the inclusive file), in accordance with the theory.

Let me generalize. In diachronic cases, updating is a prerequisite for enrolling a previous thought into the current train of reasoning. Once updating has been factored in, there no longer is any temptation to regard the premisses of the reasoning as involving distinct mental files or modes of presentation.

This generalization provides an obvious solution to the difficulty raised by Ninan in the passage I already quoted:

Suppose that, at time t_1, I look at my watch and think to myself, *It's 1:00pm now*. Later (at t_2) I come to think, *Actually, it wasn't 1:00pm then; I forgot to change my watch after the flight*. Intuitively, I changed my mind between t_1 and t_2 about whether it was 1:00pm at the time in question. But my initial thought employs a *now*-file μ_1, while my later thought employs a *then*-file μ_2. According to Recanati, μ_1 and μ_2 are distinct files or modes of presentation. But then why should this count as a change of mind? Normally, if I ascribe a property to an object o while thinking of it under mode of presentation m_1 and then later ascribe an incompatible property to o while thinking of it under a distinct mode of presentation m_2, I do not thereby count as changing my mind.   (Ninan 2015: 370)

Change of mind occurs only when there is diachronic disagreement between the subject and his former self. Disagreement requires a common content for the parties to disagree about, and that common content is reached through conversion in diachronic cases. I analyse Ninan's example as follows:

t_1: It's 1:00 p.m. now
    ↓ *conversion*
t_2: (a) **It was 1:00 p.m. then**   (updated thought)
      (b) **Actually, it wasn't 1:00 p.m. then;**   (new thought)
      I forgot to change my watch after the flight

There is a clear inconsistency between the updated thought 'it was 1:00 p.m. then', which results from converting the file in the initial thought 'It's 1:00 p.m. now', and the new thought which supersedes the updated thought when the subject realizes that he forgot to change his watch: 'it wasn't 1:00 p.m. then'. The contents of (a) and (b) are 'incompatible in the appropriate sense' (Ninan 2015: 370) and they give rise to genuine disagreement: the subject has changed his mind.

Does the subject entertain contradictory thoughts at t_2? That would be a very unfortunate result, it seems. Change of mind is diachronic, not synchronic, disagreement. So why represent the subject as holding two contradictory thoughts at t_2? I respond that the notion of 'holding a thought' is ambiguous. Among the thoughts that are entertained, only some are held assertively. Thoughts that are held assertively at a given time may no longer be at a later time. Thus the thought 'It's 1:00 p.m. now' is held assertively at t_1. At t_2 it is updated to 'It was 1:00 p.m. then', and it is no longer held assertively: the subject *retracts* (rather than *asserts*) that thought at t_2. This does not prevent the thought from being entertained (in its updated form) at t_2. As Bergson pointed out, you can't retract or reject a thought without entertaining it. So there is a sense in which the subject entertains two contradictory thoughts at t_2, when he changes his mind; but only one of the two thoughts is mentally asserted.

5.3. Dynamic Files

It is not the same thing to think of a time as *then* and to think of it as *now*. As John Perry pointed out many years ago, the actions one takes as a result of thinking one thing (e.g. 'the meeting starts now') are systematically different from the actions one takes as a result of thinking the other ('the meeting started then'). Given the constitutive connection between thought and action, we need to acknowledge fine-grained thought constituents which distinguish *now*-thoughts from *then*-thoughts even when the time referred to is the same (Perry 2000). Mental files based on specific ER relations are meant to play that role (the FC role). Yet to account for cross-temporal cases we have to make room for coarse-grained modes of presentation enabling the mixing of temporal perspectives (e.g. the simultaneous exploitation of memory and perception). Coarse-grained modes of presentation correspond, in my framework, to *composite files based on multiple ER relations* (and generated through incremental conversion). So it is true that the FC role requires fine-grained files, while the TI role demands coarse-grained files, but thanks to the mechanism of incremental conversion we can have both; and it is a noteworthy feature of my account that it appeals to both types of file.

This invites an objection, however. Since, to solve the problem raised by cross-modal and cross-temporal TI, I have to make room for coarse-grained files, based on multiple ER relations, in addition to the fine-grained files based on specific ER relations, it is natural to wonder whether one might not do everything with the coarse-grained files, and dispense with the fine-grained files altogether. Instead of starting with fine-grained files based on specific ER relations, and generating the coarse-grained files through the mechanism of incremental conversion, we might start from the other end. At the other end we find *maximally inclusive* files. I call them *encyclopedia entries*: files that are hospitable to information derived through *any* ER relation available to the subject. Even though, in *Mental Files,* I describe them as based on a 'higher-order' ER relation to the reference and therefore as still in line with my indexical model (which construes all files as based on ER relations), I agree with Ball (2015) that they are not *practically* indexical: they are independent of any particular contextual relation to the refer-ence and are therefore eminently stable, in contrast to the indexical files based on specific ER relations. They are what Perry calls 'detached files'. Encyclopedia entries are more like names than they are like indexicals (and indeed, I want to say that encyclopedia entries are the type of file associated with proper names). The suggestion, then, is that we should start with these maximally inclusive files, independent of any specific contextual relation, and distinguish different stages in their evolution.

That is the approach which Papineau (2006, 2013) advocates. When I first encounter an object, he says, I open an encyclopedia entry (a stable file) for that object. For the time being, my only relation to it may be demonstrative/perceptual, but soon I will be in a position to gain information from it through additional ER relations (e.g. testimony). So-called demonstrative files, on this view, are nothing but stages in the development of namelike files—the only files we need. No conversion needs to take place, because the encyclopedia entry is there from the start.[4]

Both Ball (2015) and Ninan (2015) concur with Papineau. They think we can do everything with lasting files based on indefinitely many ER relations. Ball shows in some detail that a 'names-only' system can be used to represent indexical information (about time, in his example), without any need for a specialized indexical file. If the two systems (the names-only system and the indexical system) are equivalent, as Ball suggests, why not go for Papineau's 'simpler view' (only encyclopedia entries)? As Ninan (2015: 373) puts it,

---

[4] Here is a verbatim quote from Papineau: 'When I first encounter some item perceptually, I open a potentially permanent file in which to accumulate information about that item. That file outlasts the original encounter, and the same file is reactivated when I remember the relevant item or re-encounter it. The information earlier acquired is thus automatically available on those later occasions, and can be added to when new facts are acquired, without any need for any multiplication of files. (See Papineau 2006.) On this view, the files that we open on first perceptual encounters, and in general on coming into any contact with any new item of thought, are *name-like*. They are designed to be permanent repositories of information about the item in question, and are not dependent on any particular sources of information about that object. In this respect they are akin to Recanati's "encyclopaedic" files, whose function is to gather information about some referent from whatever sources offer themselves.' (Papineau 2013: 168–9).

'once we have the stable relations and piles, what need is there for unstable relations and files proper?'[5]

Onofri mentions that I have myself taken a step in that direction (in addition to the distinction between files and piles already in *Mental Files*). In 'Mental Files: Replies to My Critics' (Recanati 2013b), in the special issue of *Disputatio* dedicated to my book, I introduced a numerical index on files which corresponds to the fact that they are related by conversion. Coindexing means that two files belong to the same *sequence of files*, what we may call a 'dynamic file'. Why, then, should we not try to do everything with dynamic files (and their stages)? Note that encyclopedia entries are intrinsically dynamic: their function is to exploit all the ER relations available, so they are designed to grow new information links whenever possible. Instead of describing conversion as an operation external to files, we can therefore take a more dynamic approach and view incremental conversion as internally generated in virtue of the function of encyclopedia entries.

I am, myself, all in favour of such a dynamic approach. Consider a descriptive name like Evans's 'Julius'. It is associated with a *descriptive file*, a type of file which has interesting properties and is worth investigating in its own right. 'Neptune' also started its life as a descriptive name, but acquaintance with the reference has led to conversion of the descriptive file initially associated with the name into a regular encyclopedia entry based on ER relations to the reference. So the descriptive file at the source of the name may be viewed as a stage in the dynamic evolution of an encyclopedia entry. As Stalnaker fancifully points out, the descriptive name 'Julius' might evolve in the same way:

What [Evans] did was to establish a semantic link between the name 'Julius' and a certain person. The role of the description ['the inventor of the zip'] was to fix the reference, not to be part of giving the meaning.

---

[5] 'Piles' were my first attempt to deal with what I now call 'dynamic files'.

[. . .] 'How did Whitcomb L. Judson [the actual inventor of the zip] ever come to be called "Julius"?' someone may someday ask. The historians answer: 'Years ago, a philosopher, in concocting an example, gave that name to the inventor of the zip, and it later came to light that Judson was the one he had named.'   (Stalnaker 2003: 198)

Or consider the *deferential file* a person might associate with a name overheard in a conversation: when the person hears more about the referent of the name the deferential file will be converted into a regular encyclopedia entry. These examples show that we need an analysis with two levels: the local, static level, and the global, dynamic level. The dynamic level is essential for understanding informational updating, but also for understanding communication, if it is accepted that dynamic files (sequences of files) can be interpersonal as well as intrapersonal (Prosser forthcoming).[6]

So I agree that we need dynamic files, and I agree that encyclopedia entries are intrinsically dynamic. As a result, I have no objection to Papineau's dynamic picture. What I reject is only the idea that we should *dispense with fine-grained files and with operations like conversion*. I think the best way to account for dynamic files themselves is by analysing them as chained sequences of more or less fine-grained, static files.[7] We need the static files, in particular, to make sense of dynamic phenomena like fusion and fission of files.

As Prosser points out:

The problems resulting from fission and fusion for modes of presentation are very similar to those that arise for psychological continuity theories of personal identity. For every type of solution on offer for personal identity there will be a corresponding type of solution for modes of presentation. My own view is that the best solution is given by stage theory (Sider 1996, 2001; Hawley 2001).   (Prosser forthcoming: 18)

---

[6] On interpersonal dynamic files, see Chapter 8.

[7] Dynamic files are necessarily coarse-grained, but file stages, or static files, may be fine-grained *or* coarse-grained. Composite files are coarse-grained, yet static.

Assuming that persons are both dynamic continuants (space-time worms) and stages, what is basic? Because the dynamic view which takes continuants as basic has the unpalatable consequence that distinct individuals can be located in the same place at the same time (Lewis 1976), Sider suggests that person stages should be construed as basic (Sider 1996, 2001: chapter 5). That is the view I take in the case of mental files, though not for the same reason. I take modes of presentation (what plays the FC role) to be static files or *file-stages*, and I take such files to undergo dynamic operations such as conversion, incremental conversion, fusion (file merging), fission (file splitting), and so on. Sequences of files related by such operations are dynamic files. These operations do not preserve file identity in the strict, Leibnizian sense: in contrast to identity, dynamic continuity between files is an intransitive relation, just like dynamic continuity between person stages.

Let us consider an example (already mentioned). At t_1, I see a certain object and open a demonstrative file DEM$_1$ about it: 'that thing'. At t_2, the object I have been in contact with since t_1 disintegrates, but the demonstrative file persists because, as a result of taking a certain drug, I hallucinate the continued presence of the object. There is an issue whether or not the file continues to refer after t_2. I think it does not, since the presuppositions of the demonstrative file are doubly violated.[8] At t_3 a doubt occurs to me and I wonder whether the object I remember seeing at the beginning of the episode (t_1) is really the same as the object that I (mistakenly) take myself to seeing at t_3. Rational doubts about identity necessarily involve two distinct mental files, and here the two files result from splitting DEM$_1$, which is replaced by a memory demonstrative

---

[8] The deployment of a demonstrative file presupposes both that there is an object to which the subject is attending, and that whatever the subject is attending to is the same thing she has attended to in previous deployments of the file. Both presuppositions are violated in this example. If the object had been 'switched' at t_2 rather than disintegrated, only the second presupposition would be violated, but the subject would still fail to refer (through confusion).

(referring to the object initially seen) and a perceptual demonstrative (purporting to refer to the object currently seen). So there are three files in this example: DEM_1, the demonstrative file opened at t_1 and maintained until t_3 (despite the disappearance of the object at t_2); MEM, the memory demonstrative file deployed at t_3; and DEM_2, the new demonstrative file, also deployed at t_3. Both MEM and DEM_2 result from splitting DEM_1 at t_3. At t_1, DEM_1 referred to the object o the subject was then in visual contact with. At t_2, DEM_1 did not refer to anything. At t_3, DEM_1 went out of existence, and two new files were deployed: MEM inherits the reference of DEM_1 at t_1, so it refers to o (and inherits the information in DEM_1 at t_1), while DEM_2 fails to refer because the subject is hallucinating.

It seems to me that there is as much dynamic continuity between DEM_1 (as deployed between t_2 and t_3, while hallucinating) and DEM_2 as there is between DEM_1 (as deployed at t_1) and MEM. Such dynamic continuity can't ground identity, for if it did, we would have both $DEM_1 = DEM_2$ and $DEM_1 = $ MEM. That would entail that MEM $= DEM_2$, which is impossible since rational doubts about identity (like the doubt harboured at t_3) necessarily involve two distinct mental files. This suggests that we should resist Ninan's claim (following Frege in 'The Thought' and Evans in 'Understanding Demonstratives') that:

the mode of presentation associated with *today* on day d is the same as the mode of presentation associated with *yesterday* on the day after d. If modes of presentation are mental files, then the mental file involved in a *today*–thought on d should be the same file involved in a *yesterday*-thought on the following day.   (Ninan 2015: 371)[9]

The modes of presentation are 'the same' only in a weak, dynamic sense which does not correspond to Leibnizian identity. In the strict

---

[9] Ninan himself qualifies that claim, in the passage partially quoted in note 11. There he says that Frege and Evans were 'wrong about this particular example' (Ninan 2015: 371n).

sense they are not the same: they are distinct modes of presentation even though they are stages of one and the same evolving file.

5.4. Rational Relationships and Proper Dynamic Files

Ninan could respond by pointing out that not all dynamic relations between stages matter; what matters are only those that support 'rational relationships'. As he puts it:

The notion of a mode of presentation was introduced in part to describe what we might call rational relationships between beliefs. Since a rational agent can believe that Hesperus is bright without believing that Phosphorus is bright, these beliefs must have different contents, and so the two modes of presentation for Venus must be different. Here we focus on the rational relationships between the beliefs of an agent at a single time. But we can also consider the rational relationships between two beliefs of an agent that are held at different times. The reason for thinking that my belief (*It is now 1:00pm*) at t_1 and my belief (*It was not 1:00pm then*) at t_2 involve the same mode of presentation is precisely that there is rational relationship between these two beliefs: they are incompatible, which partly explains why I count as having changed my mind between t_1 and t_2.   (Ninan 2015: 371–2)

If we focus on that subset of dynamic relations that qualify as 'rational relationships' in Ninan's sense, it is not so clear that they can't ground identity for modes of presentation. Arguably, in my example, there is such a relationship between DEM$_1$ at t_1 and MEM, but *not* between DEM$_1$ at t_2 and DEM$_2$. So perhaps we can say, on that basis, that DEM$_1$ (at t_1) and MEM are the same mode of presentation, while DEM$_1$ (at t_2) and DEM$_2$ are not the same mode of presentation (thus blocking the unwelcome consequence that MEM = DEM$_2$).

Now what is the special relationship which holds between DEM$_1$ at t_1 and MEM but not between DEM$_1$ at t_2 and DEM$_2$? It is something like this. A memory file *inherits its reference* (and its content) from the perceptual file it derives from.[10] The memory file is referentially dependent upon the perceptual file, so they are bound to corefer (assuming the perceptual file refers). On that basis, we could say, following Ninan (and Evans), that the perceptual file and the subsequent memory file count as the same mode of presentation because they bear the appropriate rational relation to each other, a relation that rules out any possibility of referential divergence. The situation is different with DEM_1 and DEM_2 because DEM_2 results from the *fission* of DEM_1. Whenever fission (or, for that matter, fusion) is involved, there always is the possibility that one of the twin files (or both) refer while the inclusive file fails to refer (Ball 2015: 365).

Recall that, in Chapters 2 and 3, I drew a distinction between a strong and a weak form of coreference *de jure* (CDJ). Fusion and fission do not support CDJ in the strong sense:

Coreference *de jure* (strong): the two occurrences corefer if either of them refers.

Coreference *de jure* (weak): the two occurrences corefer if both of them refer.

In cases of fusion and fission, the files only exhibit the weak form of coreference *de jure*: the two files are bound to corefer if they *both* refer. There is the possibility that one of the files refers while the other one fails to refer, but it is ruled out that the two files both refer while referring to different things.

If this is on the right track, then we need three levels. We need the static files (or file-stages) and the dynamic operations on them: conversion, fusion, fission, etc. This gives us the notion of a dynamic file. Then we can distinguish two kinds of dynamic files:

---

[10] As Dummett points out, 'I cannot separate the knowledge I suppose myself to have now [through memory] from the knowledge I surely had at the past time [through perception]. For the former is derived from the latter; more exactly, it simply *is* the knowledge I had as an eyewitness, maintained in being' (Dummett 1993: 414–15). This is similar to Burge's well-known take on 'preservative memory' (Burge 1993, 2003a; see Matthen 2010 for critical discussion relevant to what follows).

those which do and those which do not support Ninan's 'rational relationships'. The files that do may be called the proper dynamic files. It is at the level of the proper dynamic file that we can try to capture the notion of a dynamic mode of presentation which Ninan and Evans argue for, and we can do so in terms of strong CDJ. Strong coreference *de jure* between stages is a transitive relation, so it can ground the identity of (dynamic) modes of presentation of the sort Evans and Ninan are after. In contrast, weak CDJ is not transitive. For example, in fusion or fission, an inclusive file A/B may bear weak CDJ to both of the twin files A and B, while A and B do not bear weak CDJ to each other.

But, as I already pointed out (Chapter 3), it is far from clear that dynamic files *ever* exhibit strong CDJ. There are five types of dynamic file to consider: (i) deployments of the same file at different times; (ii) 'simple' conversion of one file into another (*now/then, here/there, today/yesterday* . . .); (iii) incremental conversion (multiplication of ER relations); (iv) fusion; (v) fission. Fusion and fission only support weak CDJ, as we have seen. There always is the possibility that one of the twin files (or both) refer(s) while the inclusive file fails to refer. The same thing is true of incremental conversion. The incremented file may fail to refer through violation of the uniqueness presupposition (to the effect that the various ER relations converge on the same object), even if the initial file (pre-incremental conversion) succeeded in referring. More interestingly, in case (i) too we find weak rather than strong CDJ. That is what the example of DEM_1 shows: at t_1 DEM_1 refers to o, while it fails to refer at t_2. So two deployments of the same file at different times are not coreferential *de jure* in the strong sense; they are only bound to refer to the same thing if they *both* refer (weak CDJ).

It seems, then, that simple conversion, illustrated by Ninan's *now/then* example, would be *the only case* of a proper dynamic file, exhibiting strong CDJ. It would be an *exception* to the generalization that dynamic files only support weak CDJ. But do we really need such an exception?

One may be sceptical of any account that creates too big a gap between simple and incremental conversion. Is it true that simple conversion (e.g. Ninan's *now/then* example) supports strong CDJ while incremental conversion only supports weak CDJ? I am not sure. It is well known that simple temporal conversion supports strong CDJ only if the thinker has managed to 'keep track of time' (see Kaplan 1989a, Evans 1981). Rip van Winkle is the case of a thinker who has not kept track of time, and whose temporal file about the previous day is confused. But the requirement that the thinker keep track of time introduces an artificial asymmetry between the case of simple conversion and incremental conversion. The sort of confusion which may give rise to reference failure in cases of incremental conversion (or fusion) corresponds to cases in which the uniqueness condition is not satisfied: the various ER relations do not converge on the same object. That is why incremental conversion only supports weak CDJ. But if we ruled out such cases by adding a condition analogous to the time-tracking requirement, e.g. the requirement that the subject 'keep track' of the object throughout the dynamic operation, then incremental conversion would turn out to support strong CDJ as well.

I conclude that it is not obvious that *any* dynamic file (without the help of extra conditions, like the time-tracking requirement) support strong CDJ. My conjecture is that only *synchronic deployments of the same file* do so. If that conjecture is correct, then we cannot use proper dynamic files (based on a transitive relation) to ground the identity of dynamic modes of presentation, because there are *no* 'proper' dynamic files. Dynamic files only support weak CDJ, and weak CDJ is not a transitive relation.

5.5. *Failsafe Updating*

An anonymous reader for Oxford University Press provided an interesting response on behalf of Ninan. Rip van Winkle has lost track of time, but even he can think of the day at the source of his memory as 'that day'. The conversion from 'Today is F' to 'That day was F', where 'that day' invokes a memory of day d, runs no risk of generating confusion. It is failsafe. Because the memory demonstrative 'that day' refers to the day of the original experience (that which is recorded in the memory), it automatically inherits the reference of 'today' in the initial thought (Perry 1997). As the reader puts it:

If I remember a certain time, then I can think about that time whether or not I have managed to 'keep track of time'. Suppose Rip van Winkle falls asleep on day d. He sleeps for twenty years, and then wakes up, thinking he's slept for eight hours. Rip has lost track of time. But, intuitively, Rip can still think about d. He can think that it was sunny on d, by thinking, 'It was sunny on *that day*' intending the complex demonstrative to refer to d, a representation of which he retains in memory. Rip will also think, 'It was sunny yesterday' since he thinks that d was the day before the present day. But we should distinguish his true 'that day' thoughts about d from his false 'yesterday' thoughts about the day before his waking.[11]

I grant that Rip van Winkle can think of the day at the source of his memory as 'that day'. That is what Perry calls a 'backup character' (Perry 1997: 36). But I maintain that, *when he wakes up*, Rip does not think of d under that character. Rather, he deploys a composite file, based on both memory and time-tracking, and refers through it when he says: 'Yesterday was nice'. The day d is then thought of *both* as the day remembered *and* as the previous day. Rip will move to a *pure* memory demonstrative such as 'that day' (Perry's backup character), and succeed in referring to d, only if he comes to suspect that he is confused and has lost track

---

[11] Reader B, 'Comments on *Mental Files in Flux* by François Recanati'. Ninan makes the same point in a footnote: 'If I think *today is warm* on a certain day, then in order to think the very same thought on the next day I must think an appropriate thought of the form *that day was warm*. The corresponding *yesterday*-thought is not the very same thought, simply because I might fail to realize that "that day" was yesterday' (Ninan 2015: 371n).

of time. He will then split the composite file and create two distinct files, the 'that day' file (a memory file) and the 'yesterday' file (a file based on time-tracking). In general, splitting one's file is the only cure for confusion; it is the price to pay to achieve successful reference. In Rip's circumstances, reference *simpliciter* is out of reach before fission occurs—only partial or confused reference is available prior to splitting the composite file.

If we accept that Rip van Winkle fails to refer *simpliciter* to *d* when, upon waking up, he thinks 'Yesterday was nice', we have to accept that in this case at least, simple conversion does not support strong CDJ. Rip's initial thought, before he falls asleep, is 'Today is nice' (or 'Today was nice', since that is the end of the day). When he wakes up, the thought is updated and the update yields a shift in truth-value: the initial thought was true, but the updated thought after conversion is neither true nor false. It is confused.

Still, the reader has a point: even if Rip's 'yesterday'-thought is irreducibly confused, it seems that the backup 'that day'-thought which he may entertain *after* splitting his composite file cannot but corefer with the initial 'today'-thought. If that is right, then failsafe instances of conversion like Ninan's *now*/*then* update give rise to dynamic files that do support strong CDJ:

'*Today*' thoughts on day *d* are not rationally linked to 'yesterday' thoughts on day *d+1*; rather, they are rationally linked to appropriate 'that day' thoughts on day *d+1* (and on subsequent days as well). If this is right, then I think that there is a class of dynamic files that support strong CDJ. And if that's right, then there is a class of dynamic files which are 'proper' files, i.e. files that are unified by a transitive relation.[12]

But why think that the different types of simple conversion (*today*/*yesterday*, *now*/*then*, *here*/*there* . . .) work differently? Why think that some are safe while others are risky? As far as I can tell,

---

[12] Reader B, 'Comments on *Mental Files in Flux*'.

the argument runs as follows. *Today/yesterday* conversion rests on time-tracking, and the time-tracking system can malfunction. That is what the Rip van Winkle example shows. *Here/there* conversion similarly rests on place-tracking, and it is easy to imagine situations of confusion arising from some malfunctioning of the place-tracking system. But there are cases of temporal conversion that involve no risk of confusion, namely the cases in which the subject is left with an isolated memory corresponding to a past experience he or she is totally unable to locate. The subject's inability to locate the experience means that the time-tracking system does not operate or at least fails to yield any result. As the OUP reader points out after Perry (1997), the subject can *still* think of the day of the remembered experience as 'that day', in a purely attributive manner ('that day, whatever it is'). Because the temporal reference is purely attributive, it seems that no mistake can occur: temporal reference is immune to error through mis-identification when the operations of the time-tracking system are suspended. So there are two types of temporal conversion: if the time-tracking system is operative, misidentification of the time of the original experience is possible and updating to that time is risky; but if the time-tracking system is suspended or yields no result, no misidentification of the time of the original experience can occur. In such a case, one incurs no risk whatsoever when one moves from 'Today is F' to 'That day was F'. That is failsafe updating, and it supports strong coreference *de jure*.

This is an interesting idea, but I don't think it really works. Even in the sort of case at issue, I would maintain, the subject locates the experience *in his or her past*. The difference between that case and the others is simply that the subject locates the experience in his or her past in a fully *unspecific* manner. The subject has no idea *when* the original experience took place, but this is compatible with holding that the experience took place *at some point or other in his or her life*. Now this much is enough to generate a risk of error.

Quasi-memory is the imaginary case in which the remembered experience did not take place in the remembering subject's past, but in the past of *some other subject*.[13] For example, we can imagine that neurosurgeons, by connecting the subject's brain to the brain of someone else, have managed to implant in the subject's mind apparent memories that do not derive from his or her own prior experiences. This case is fictional, of course, but so is the Rip van Winkle example. More realistic is the case in which the subject S_1 heard of the experience of some other subject S_2 (who may have described the scene to S_1 in vivid detail) and unconsciously fabricated an apparent memory of that experience, which S_1 now wrongly self-ascribes (on the basis of the apparent memory). In this type of example, we find the ingredients for a truth-value shift. S_2 enjoys an experience which she reports as 'It is F now' or 'Today is F'. As a result, S_1 forms an apparent memory reportable as 'It was F then' or 'That day was F'. Even if S_1 feels unable to place the remembered experience correctly, she can't help locating it loosely in her own past. In general, it is *presupposed* that the causal source of a memory is an experience located in the rememberer's past: that presupposition is constitutive of how episodic memory works. If the presupposition is false, thoughts based on a memory such as 'That day was F' are confused, and fail to carry a definite truth-value. 'That day was F' roughly means 'The day of the experience was F' (Perry 1997), and that is like 'The King of France is bald': 'the experience' refers to the unique experience which is both the causal source of the memory *and* something that occurred in the subject's past. In quasi-memory and related cases nothing fits that description, just as nothing fits the description 'the King of France'. In both cases, presupposition failure yields reference failure.

[13] That sort of case was introduced by Shoemaker (1970) in connection with immunity to error through misidentification, and discussed by Evans (1982) among many others. See Recanati 2007: chapter 21.

These examples reveal an important fact about temporal updating: in the intrapersonal case (personal memory), it is *never* without risk. The subject's time-tracking system which is suspended in the failsafe cases is part of a *larger system* whose role is to enable the subject to locate the experiences recorded in his or her memories. That system can malfunction even though the time-tracking system narrowly understood is off.

Let me not be misunderstood. I am not denying that there is a purely demonstrative type of mode of presentation *that day* (in the sense of 'type' spelled out in the Preface, p. xvi) which exclusively targets the day of the remembered experience, irrespective of its putative temporal location. Such a type is clearly available. But I think it is not at work in ordinary cases of temporal updating. Ordinary subjects cannot help but locate, however vaguely, the experiences recorded in their apparent memories. Whether or not the time-tracking system is in operation, temporal reference proceeds through two distinct routes whose convergence is presupposed: the causal route from the memory to its actual source, and the interpretive route from the memory to some more or less definite region of the subject's autobiography. If the routes do not converge—if the source of the memory is not located in the relevant region—there is failure of reference. Such failure of reference is almost always possible, even if the subject is left with an isolated memory; so, I am inclined to maintain the generalization that temporal conversion only supports weak coreference *de jure*. There are exceptions, admittedly, but they don't affect the overall picture.[14]

---

[14] In Gibbard's example, *'that woman was happy then'*, discussed in Section A.5 in the Appendix to Part II, the mode of presentation *then* works in a purely attributive manner: 'Ben's word *then* voices, in this utterance, the concept of whenever this letter was written' (Gibbard 2012: 267). Similarly, I can look at an old photograph of Paris and think: *'Streets were crowded then'*, without having the faintest idea when the photograph was taken. Such cases, involving attributive uses of indexicals, conform to Ninan's description, but they do not illustrate how temporal conversion works in general.

Part II

Interpersonal Coordination
of Mental Files

6

Indexical Thought

6.1. Mental Indexicality

THERE was a time when people took indexicality to be a property of language, and of language exclusively. Thought itself, they believed, *could not be* indexical (any more than it could be ambiguous). Then came the discovery of 'the essential indexical'. Prior, Castañeda, Perry, Kaplan, and Lewis put forward examples in which removing the indexicals from a sentence changes the nature of the thought that is expressed.[1] 'In these cases', Stalnaker says (1981: 133), 'there seems to be no way to eliminate the indexical element in the expression [. . .] of the attitude without distorting the content'. This seems to establish that *the thought expressed by uttering an indexical sentence is itself indexical.* Indexicality is 'essential' to the extent that it is a feature of *thought itself,* not merely of the linguistic means through which it is expressed.

What was the argument which had convinced so many philosophers, before the Castañeda–Perry shift, that thought itself could not be indexical (or ambiguous)? It is the following. Indexicality,

---

[1] See Castañeda's and Perry's respective collections of papers on the topic (Castañeda 1999, Perry 1993, 2000), as well as Prior 1959, Kaplan 1989a, and Lewis 1979.

like ambiguity, has to do with the *relation* between the sentences we utter and the thoughts we thereby express. If we abstract from the relation, by considering the thought itself (one of the relata), the notions of ambiguity or indexicality no longer apply. It is, therefore, a *category mistake* to ask whether thought itself is, or might be, indexical.

Consider ambiguity first, to see how the argument works. Ambiguity is a property that is instantiated when the same sentence, or what superficially looks like the same sentence, expresses distinct thoughts. If we abstract from the linguistic expression of thought and consider the thoughts themselves, no room is left for ambiguity: the thoughts themselves cannot be ambiguous, only their linguistic expression can. As Jerry Fodor (one of the early opponents of both mental ambiguity and mental indexicality) puts it, 'whereas it's thoughts that equivocal sentences equivocate between [...], there doesn't seem to be anything comparable around that could serve to disequivocate thought' (Fodor 2003: 56).

Were this argument against mental ambiguity correct, it would apply to mental indexicality as well. Indexicality is a property that is instantiated when a given sentence expresses distinct thoughts in different contexts and does not express any thought independent of context. If we abstract from the linguistic expression of thought and consider the thoughts themselves, no room is left for indexicality. As we might put it, paraphrasing Fodor: whereas it is thoughts that indexical sentences express with respect to context, there doesn't seem to be anything comparable that thoughts themselves could express with respect to context. Thoughts don't express anything—they are *what* we express.

The argument begs the question, by presupposing a specific conception of thought as necessarily endowed with absolute truth-conditions. Indexical sentences are said to 'express different thoughts in different contexts', because their truth-conditions vary across contexts. But the variation in truth-conditions is not sufficient to establish that indexical sentences express different thoughts in different contexts, *unless* one assumes the Fregean conception of thought as absolutely truth-evaluable. That conception is not inevitable, however. There is an alternative conception of thought, which Hintikka ascribes to Aristotle and the Stoics and recommends as 'very natural':[2]

It is obvious that the sentence, 'It is raining', as uttered by me today, is made true or false by a set of facts different from those that verified or falsified my utterance yesterday, 'It is raining'. But it is very natural to say that in some sense the state of mind or attitude toward my environment that is expressed by the two utterances is the same. The facts to which yesterday's utterance refers are referred to today by the sentence, 'It was raining yesterday'. But the 'state of mind' that this utterance appears to express seems to be entirely different from that expressed by yesterday's present-tense utterance, 'It is raining'. [. . .] Hence the idea that spoken words are symbols for unspoken thoughts encourages the idea that one and the same temporally indefinite form of words expresses one and the same belief or opinion at the different times when it is uttered. (Hintikka 1973: 85)

Indexical thoughts may thus be characterized as *thoughts whose (absolute) truth-conditions are not fixed once and for all but depend upon the context.* When I think 'it is raining' at t, the thought is true iff it is raining at t. When I think *the same thought* at t', the thought is true iff it is raining at t'. That is, basically, Lewis' approach to the *de se* (Lewis 1979). According to his interpretation of the Perry example, Heimson and Hume both think 'I am Hume'. They think *the same thought*. But the (absolute) truth-conditions of the thought depend on the context of tokening.

---

[2] Stalnaker finds the alternative conception 'less natural' than the standard, Fregean conception of thoughts as absolutely evaluable (Stalnaker 2008: 50). Those acquainted with the earlier tradition, like Hintikka and Prior, find the alternative conception of thought as natural, if not more. In their book *The Development of Logic* (1962: 165) Kneale and Kneale describe the Frege–Russell conception as 'very strange' in comparison to the older conception held by the Stoics. For a comparison (and a historical overview) of the two conceptions, see Prior 1957: 104–22.

When thought by Hume, the thought is true iff Hume is Hume; when thought by Heimson it is true iff Heimson is Hume. In other words, the thought is true 'at' Hume, but false 'at' Heimson, just as 'it is raining' is true at t but false at t'.

Let us now reconsider the argument against mental indexicality. It says that indexicality is a *relational* matter: it is a property of the expression relation between sentences and thoughts. If we look at thoughts themselves and abstract from their linguistic expression, the expression relation disappears from view, and the notion of indexicality no longer applies (so the argument goes). But if, following Hintikka and Lewis, we reject the Fregean stipulation regarding the absolute truth-evaluability of thoughts, we can respond to the argument by pointing out that *there is* a relation which we can use to make sense of the idea of mental indexicality. It is the relation between the thought and its (absolute) truth-conditions. The thought 'it is raining' has different truth-conditions when it is thought at t and when it is thought at t'. Likewise, for Lewis, the thought 'I am Hume' has different truth-conditions when thought by Hume and when thought by Heimson. The thought/truth-conditions pairing is relative to context, and this is sufficient to make the notion of indexicality applicable to the mental realm.

This result can be achieved *even if we allow for a Fregean view of content as absolutely truth-evaluable*. For Frege, a complete thought content can only be true or false, *tertium non datur*.[3] It cannot be true at t and false at t', or true at x but false at y. Since the 'thought' that it is raining is true (when entertained on a rainy day) *and* false (when entertained on a sunny day), it follows that it is not a genuine thought—a complete content—by Fregean standards.

---

[3] 'A thought is not true at one time and false at another, but it is either true or false, *tertium non datur*. The false appearance that a thought can be true at one time and false at another arises from an incomplete expression. A complete proposition or expression of a thought must also contain a time datum' (Frege 1967a: 338; quoted in Evans 1985: 350).

We can *accept* that stipulation (and the Fregean notion of thought based on it), and still make sense of the alternative notion of thought. As I pointed out in several places, the two notions of thought are compatible. The *complete content* of an utterance of 'It is raining' (what *Frege* calls the thought) arguably depends upon two factors: one internal and one external. The internal factor is the (Aristotelian) thought that is expressed: 'the state of mind or attitude toward [the] environment', as Hintikka puts it. The external factor is the time at which the (Aristotelian) thought is expressed or entertained. Without the external factor, no complete thought content in Frege's sense would be expressed. But the internal factor has an important role to play: it is meant to capture what is common to all of those who think 'It is raining' (and behave accordingly) in their respective contexts.

At this point we can help ourselves to a useful situation-theoretic notion: that of an 'Austinian proposition' (Barwise 1989, Barwise and Etchemendy 1987, Recanati 1996, 1997a, 2000, 2007). An Austinian proposition has two components. One is a relativized proposition—something that has 'truth-at'-conditions. In a possible worlds semantics it can be modelled as a set of centred worlds, as suggested by Lewis. Let the proposition that one is Hume be such a relativized proposition, true at Hume but false at Heimson. The other component of the Austinian proposition is the index relative to which the relativized proposition is to be evaluated (the relevant 'centre'). In the case at hand the index is either Hume or Heimson, depending on the context, so this gives us two Austinian propositions:

<Hume, the relativized proposition that one is Hume>
<Heimson, the relativized proposition that one is Hume>

In contrast to the relativized proposition, which has only 'truth-at'-conditions (it is true at certain indices and false at others), the Austinian proposition has *absolute* truth-conditions: it is true iff the relativized proposition is true at the relevant index. In this framework, we get the two levels of content we need to capture mental indexicality. The Austinian proposition, with its absolute truth-conditions, is the complete content. It determines a set of possible worlds—the worlds in which the Austinian proposition is true. The relativized proposition is the psychological content—the subjective or internal aspect of content.[4]

6.2. *Thought Vehicles*

Perry locates indexicality not in the content of belief but in the *belief state* through which the content is apprehended; or, more accurately, in the relation between the content and the belief state. Hume and Heimson are in the same belief state, for Perry, but the contents of their beliefs are different. One believes that Hume is Hume, the other believes that Heimson is Hume. Distinct contents are presented to them under the same mode of presentation. It is also possible for the same content to be presented under distinct modes of presentation, as in Kaplan's 'my pants are on fire'/'his pants are on fire' example. Indexicality goes together with these possibilities (same state, different contents; or different states, same content).[5]

Some philosophers are unhappy with this appeal to belief states or modes of presentation. In the seventies, neo-Fregeans such as John McDowell and Gareth Evans launched an attack on the

[4] In the new framework Stalnaker has developed for thinking about these matters there is something similar to Austinian propositions: Stalnaker represents belief states by means of a pair consisting of a 'base world' (a world centred on the subject at the time of thought) and a set of centred worlds representing the subject's doxastic alternatives. (See Stalnaker 2008, 2014, and Ninan 2008: 63, fn. 9 on the analogy between Stalnaker's belief states and Austinian propositions.) The set of centred worlds gives us the relativized proposition, and the base world gives us the index with respect to which it is to be evaluated.

[5] See Perry's famous 'bear' example in Perry 1977: 23 (see also the postscript to that paper, pp. 30–1).

'two-component picture'.[6] They argued that the so-called 'internal component' is not an ingredient of content at all but the *vehicle*, or bearer, of content. Stalnaker takes the same line. While Perry construes belief states as having structure and involving concepts as constituents (corresponding to the structure and constituents of the sentence which expresses the state), Stalnaker insists that 'concepts, objects, senses and semantic structure are part of the means by which content is determined, and not components of the content itself' (Stalnaker 1981: 135). He complains that Perry's notion of a mode of presentation or way of thinking 'blur[s] the line between the content of a representation and the relation between the representation and its content' (Stalnaker 2008: 28). In yet another place he writes:

[Perry's] way of distinguishing content of belief from manner of believing distorts the phenomena, locating an aspect of Ralph's conception of what the world is like on the wrong side of the line. Ralph's way of representing Ortcutt is essential to the way he takes the world to be like, and not just to the manner in which he represents the world.   (Stalnaker 2006: 287)

Perry's distinction between the content of belief and the way it is believed is inspired from Kaplan's character/content distinction, but the analogy is misleading, Stalnaker argues:

The motivation for the distinction, in Kaplan's theory, as I understand it, is something like this: we need to distinguish the information conveyed or represented from the means by which it is conveyed or represented. The information conveyed in an utterance—what is said—is of course dependent on the meaning of the sentence uttered, but one cannot identify content with meaning since what is said may depend on other things as well; specifically, what is said may depend on information available in the environment of the utterance. Perry describes his distinction between objects of belief and belief states in a similar way as a

---

[6] See Recanati 1993: 191–226 for a presentation of their arguments and a response. For a classic statement of the two-component picture, see McGinn 1982.

distinction between *what* is believed and the *way* it is believed. But the point of Perry's distinction must be different, since the lesson of the examples of essentially indexical belief—the examples that motivate Perry's account—is that *indexicals are essential to the information itself and are not just part of the means used to represent it.* (Stalnaker 1981: 148, my emphasis)[7]

Let me respond to that barrage of criticism based on the content/vehicle distinction. I agree that psychological states are vehicles, and that vehicles should not be confused with the contents they carry. I also agree with Stalnaker that indexicality has got to be a feature of content, at some level. It can't be merely a matter of vehicle if the talk of 'essential indexicality' is to make any sense. But I think the Perry picture is not threatened, for the vehicles have *roles* in the cognitive economy, and these roles generate (internal) content. The vehicles are supposed to *do* certain things, which they can do only if the context in which they are deployed satisfies certain conditions. So the vehicles carry *presuppositional content*: their deployment *means* something, namely, that the context satisfies the conditions, whatever they are, on which their correct functioning relies. That aspect of the overall content of the vehicle is context-independent, in contrast to the truth-conditional content, which constitutively depends upon what I have called the external factor.[8]

---

[7] Stalnaker makes the point again in his last book: 'The original idea, implicit in the motivation for the character-content distinction, was that indexicality is a part of the means used to communicate, and is not involved in the content of the information that one is communicating. When I say, "I was born in New Jersey," the content of what I say is the same as the content of your utterance of "Stalnaker was born in New Jersey". You might in fact just be passing along the information that my statement gave you. But the phenomenon of essentially indexical belief complicates the story. My beliefs about who I am, and what time it is, seem to have the indexical element in the content of what is believed, and not just in the means used to express it' (Stalnaker 2014: 34). In the passage referred to in note 2, Kneale and Kneale criticize the claim that indexicality is a part of the means used to communicate and is not involved in the content of the information that one is communicating.

[8] Manuel Garcia-Carpintero has developed a similar, presupposition-based view over the years. See e.g. Garcia-Carpintero 2000, 2006, and 2016.

Consider, for example, referential expressions. What they contribute to the thought (construed as vehicle) is a mental file. A mental file is undoubtedly a vehicle of content—it is a mental representation, which carries referential content if all goes well. A mental file refers to some object in the environment, through epistemically rewarding relations (ER relations) that the file exploits. Since the role of a file is to track an object through some ER relation to that object, any deployment of the file will presuppose that there is some such object and that the relation obtains. For example, the deployment of a demonstrative file presupposes that the subject is perceptually tracking some object. The file may be deployed even if the contextual condition is not met and no reference is determined, but in all cases, whether successful or empty, the deployment of the file presupposes that the condition is satisfied. That presupposition has content, and that content accounts for behaviour (e.g. the subject's reaching for the non-existent object).

If two expressions (or two occurrences of the same expression) are associated for a subject with distinct files referring to the same object *a*, it will be possible for that subject to rationally accept both that *a* has a certain property and that it does not have that property, for it will not be presupposed that the two files corefer if they refer at all. If two expressions (or two occurrences of the same expression) are associated for a subject with the same file, that will be impossible. In other words, the files play the role of Frege's *senses*. Via the presuppositional content they carry, they account for the subject's rational behaviour, and, at the same time, they refer. What they refer to depends upon the environment, so the internal/external distinction applies. Which file is deployed in the subject's mind accounts for the subject's rational behaviour; that is the internal component. Which object stands in the relevant ER relations to the file at the time of deployment accounts for the reference of the file (and, arguably, for the reference of the expression associated with the file); that is the external component.

On this picture, the internal component is, indeed, a vehicle (a mental file), but a vehicle whose deployment carries presuppositional content. That content must be distinguished from the referential content also carried by the file: the object to which the file refers if the context satisfies its presuppositions. The same distinction between two aspects of content can be made for belief states, and that corresponds to Perry's distinction between what is believed and how it is believed. Just as sentences (and their constituents) have linguistic 'characters' which are functions from contexts to contents (Kaplan 1989a), Perry's belief states (and their constituents) have 'roles' (Perry 1979) or 'doxastic characters' (Perry 1997) which are also functions from contexts to contents. The roles in question provide the modes of presentation, which are used to make sense of the subject as a rational agent.

6.3. *Two Kinds of Content*

Perry's distinction between the two dimensions of content is analogous not only to Kaplan's character/content distinction, but also to that drawn in presupposition studies between what is 'at issue' and what is not.[9] There is a narrow notion of content ('what is said') which corresponds to at-issue content exclusively ('subject-matter content', as Perry calls it), not to *all* the information that is conveyed by an utterance. As Heck puts it:

Information can be conveyed by an utterance in all kinds of ways, not only by being (part of) what is said. [...] If someone says 'I am a philosopher', part of what is *conveyed* by such an utterance is that she self-consciously believes herself to be a philosopher. If someone says 'You are a philosopher', then part of what is conveyed is that she is talking to someone she thinks is a philosopher; 'She is a philosopher', that the

___

[9] For a review see Roberts et al. (2009).

person she demonstrates is female; and so forth. But this observation should not lead us to conclude that part of what is *expressed* by an utterance of 'I am a philosopher' is that the speaker self-consciously believes that she is a philosopher.   (Heck 2002: 25–6)[10]

Likewise for thought. Someone who judges 'That is red' is not thinking of the demonstrative relation in which she stands to the object she is thinking about. The thought she thinks is about the object, not about her relation to it. That, of course, is compatible with the fact that the subject is, or may be, aware of the relation. When Perry talks of the content of belief as opposed to the way of believing, it is that narrow notion of content that he has in mind. So it can be conceded to Stalnaker that how the subject represents Ortcutt 'is essential to the way he takes the world to be like'— essential to 'what he believes', in a suitably *broad* sense. Ralph thinks of Ortcutt through two distinct mental files, and the exist- ence of these two files in his mental economy means that, for him, there are two distinct persons. One he takes to be a spy, the other not. As Stalnaker puts it, 'were Ralph later to come to believe that the man he sees on the beach is also a spy, his conception of the world—the condition under which his beliefs would be true— would change' (Stalnaker 2006: 287). Following Stalnaker, we can represent Ralph's global belief state by saying that in each of his

___

[10]   Heck appeals to Burge's 1974 analysis of indexical sentences (based on the idea that they only have *conditional* truth-conditions) to account for the distinction between what an indexical utterance says and what it merely conveys. Higginbo- tham also appeals to Burge's 'normal forms for demonstrative reference and truth' (Higginbotham 2003: 103) to achieve the same result: 'All demonstrative and indexical reference [...] flows from rules of use and belongs entirely to the setting-up phase, so that the content of the rules does not enter the truth-conditions of what is said.' (Higginbotham 2003: 106). In my own work I follow the same strategy (Recanati 1988, 1993: chapter 1), and I extend it to the case of mental indexicality (Recanati 1993, 2012). Just as there are rules of use which conditionally determine the reference of indexicals and generate 'truth-conditionally irrelevant' aspects of content (e.g. the presupposition that the referent is female, or that she is the addressee), the mental files through which we refer in thought are governed by norms which also generate presuppositional content.

doxastic alternatives, there is a guy with a brown hat whom he has seen on several occasions, and who is a spy, and another guy, seen at the beach, who is not. In contrast to Stalnaker, however, Perry is not talking about Ralph's global (holistic) belief state—'what he takes the world to be like' or 'what he believes' in general—but about *the local belief state one is in when one thinks a given occurrent thought*, such as the thought 'That guy is a spy' (thinking of Ortcutt through the MAN-IN-THE-BROWN-HAT file). When Ralph assertively entertains that thought, he comes to believe something, which is true if and only if Ortcutt is a spy. The relation between the MAN-IN-THE-BROWN-HAT file in Ralph's mind and some individual in Ralph's environment determines who Ralph's thought is about, namely Ortcutt, but the thought is not about the relation; it is about Ortcutt. The relation is presupposed, rather than part of the at-issue content of the judgment.

The distinction between the two dimensions of content is ultimately a difference in *attitude*. About the diagonal propositions which, in his framework, carry the non-at-issue content about the subject's relation to what he is thinking about, Stalnaker says in various places that they are not a special kind of proposition, but correspond to a special way of determining a proposition. Commenting on Stalnaker's approach (similar to his own approach in terms of reflexive propositions), Perry remarks:

We do not generally believe the reflexive truth-conditions of our beliefs, or the diagonal propositions their truth requires. I am inclined to reserve 'believes' for propositions about the subject-matter of the person's belief, objects and properties for which the person has concepts and often words. [. . .] Still, [one can] have the following relation to [reflexive/diagonal] propositions: [one can] have a belief, with those reflexive truth-conditions. *I think that's a different attitude from belief.*   (Perry 2006: 218, emphasis mine)

As Perry says elsewhere, 'there is a difference between being able to think of a thing or person in virtue of some role it plays in one's life, and being able to articulate that role in thought or speech and think of it as the thing or person playing that role in one's life' (Perry 1997: 363; see also Perry 2001: 132). And also: 'Attunement to the relation that our self-notions have to ourselves, or our perceptions have to the object they are of, does not require belief or thought about the relation; it requires know-how, not know-ledge that' (Perry 2012a: 99). In earlier work, Perry drew a similar distinction between 'belief' and 'acceptance' (Perry 1980b). The subject believes the classical proposition which the Austinian proposition determines. For example, Heimson believes that he is Hume, a proposition that is true iff Heimson is Hume. But he does this through *accepting* the thought ('I am Hume') which is the internal component of the Austinian proposition.

7

Communication Across Contexts

7.1. Limited Accessibility: The Communication Problem

WHAT is specific to indexical thoughts is that they are, as Heck says after Burge, 'essentially context-bound' (Burge 1979: 430, Heck 2002: 12). The internal or subjective content of the thought and its objective truth-conditions come together only given a particular context. In a different context, the same subjective content will determine distinct truth-conditions.[1] So the complete thought, involving both the subjective content and the objective truth-conditions, is of 'limited accessibility': it is only accessible to the subjects located in the right context.[2] This, Perry says, is a 'benign form of limited accessibility', expressible as follows in his framework:

---

[1] 'We cannot in general, having moved to a different setting, preserve reference and perspective simultaneously' (Higginbotham 2003: 101).

[2] 'Without violating any essential principle of Frege's philosophy, [...] we may agree with Evans that "there are thoughts which one can have only because one occupies a particular position in space or time, or because one is currently perceiving an object"; [...] and by the same token, there are thoughts which only he can have, i.e. can think, who is the subject of them' (Dummett 1981: 122). 'Self-conscious Thoughts and Thoughts of recognition are Thoughts one can entertain only if one is in an appropriate context, i.e. suitably placed with respect to one's environment. The self-conscious Thought that I am a philosopher is one that only I can entertain: at

Anyone at any time can have access to any proposition. But not in any way. Anyone can believe of John Perry that he is making a mess. And anyone can be in the belief state classified by the sentence 'I am making a mess'. But only I can have that belief by being in that state.   (1979: 49)

This property of indexical thoughts creates an obvious problem with respect to communication. How can we manage to communicate such thoughts to those who are not in the right context? If the hearer entertains a thought with the same subjective content as the speaker's thought, that thought will not retain the truth-conditions the speaker's thought originally had. Were the hearer, upon understanding the speaker's first-person utterance, 'I am thirsty', to entertain the subjective content of the speaker's thought, he would thereby ascribe to himself the property of being thirsty (he would think 'I am thirsty'). Communication would fail dramatically, for the speaker meant to communicate that *she* was thirsty, not that the hearer was. To keep the truth-conditions constant across contexts as we shift from the speaker's to the hearer's point of view, we have to *adjust* the internal content of the thought, in the same way as Frege says we do in speech with the indexicals when the context changes.[3] But that means that what Heck (2002: 8) calls the *Naïve Conception of Communication*—a view that has been given many other names in the literature[4]—is incorrect.

The Naïve Conception of Communication rests on the idea that communication is the *replication* of thoughts: the thought the hearer entertains when he understands what the speaker is saying is the very thought which the speaker expressed. But in the indexical case, there is no replication, but some kind of systematic

least, it is the self-conscious Thought that *I* am a philosopher only when I entertain it' (Heck 2002: 12–13).

[3] 'If someone wants to say the same today as he expressed yesterday using the word *today*, he must replace this word with *yesterday*' (Frege 1967b: 24).

[4] Egan (2007) calls it the 'belief transfer model', Moss (2012) the 'package delivery model', and Weber (2013) the 'FedEx Model'. It is referred to in the cognitive linguistics literature as the 'conduit metaphor', after Reddy (1979).

transformation.[5] The truth-conditions can be preserved across contexts only if the internal content of the thought is modified or adjusted so as to compensate for the shift in point of view from the speaker to the hearer. It follows that the Naïve Conception is false. As Martin Davies said a long time ago:

The doctrine that in successful communication the hearer (audience) comes to have a thought with the same content as the thought expressed by the speaker obviously needs to be complicated in the case of communication using demonstratives.   (Davies 1982: 293)

What, exactly, is wrong with the Naïve Conception of Communication? Maybe what is wrong is the idea that what is communicated is a complete *thought*, including both the 'internal component' and the objective truth-conditions it contextually determines. Maybe we should say that what is communicated, and therefore replicated, is not the thought itself but *only* its truth-conditional content. As Perry once said, 'one reason we need singular propositions is to get at what we seek to preserve when we communicate with those who are in different contexts' (Perry 1988: 4).

But there are obvious counterexamples to the view that what is communicated is only the truth-conditional content (the singular proposition, in Perry's Kaplanian framework). There are cases in which understanding an utterance clearly *requires* thinking of the reference under a certain mode of presentation. Brian Loar gives the following example:

Suppose that Smith and Jones are unaware that the man being interviewed on television is someone they see on the train every morning and about whom, in that latter role, they have just been talking. Smith says 'He is a stockbroker', intending to refer to the man on television;

[5] 'We may think of the field of reference as the points in a space, and the perspectives as demonstratively established, and often egocentric, coordinate systems for the points. Reference to the same point from different perspectives is not a one-shot affair, but involves a general transformation of coordinate systems, mapping one entire set of perspectives into another' (Higginbotham 2003: 103).

Jones takes Smith to be referring to the man on the train. Now Jones, as it happens, has correctly identified Smith's referent, since the man on television is the man on the train; but he has failed to understand Smith's utterance. It would seem that, as Frege held, some 'manner of presentation' of the referent is, even on referential uses, essential to what is being communicated.   (Loar 1976: 357)[6]

Ninan (2010) gives a similar example, involving the modes of presentation under which the discourse participants think of themselves:

John says to Mary, *Hey! your pants are on fire!* Now suppose Mary does not realize John is speaking to her. What happens is that she sees someone in a mirror, and she thinks that John is talking to that person, and she comes to believe that that person's pants are on fire. As it turns out, that person *is* Mary; she just doesn't realize it. So if she accepts John's utterance, she will come to have a third person *de re* belief about herself to the effect that her pants are on fire. But even though Mary forms this *de re* belief about herself, there is clearly an important sense in which she hasn't understood what John said, for she hasn't realized what it is that he was trying to get her to believe. John's communicative intention will not be realized unless Mary forms the relevant *de se* belief.   (Ninan 2010: 560–1)[7]

As these examples establish, the preservation of truth-conditional content is a major constraint which the communicative process has to satisfy, but there are other constraints—communication is not

---

[6] Heck (2002: 32–3) uses Perry's 'Enterprise' example to make essentially the same point. In Perry's example, there is a very long ship that can be seen through two windows (the bow through window A, the stern through window B). Neither the speaker not the hearer suspects that it is the same (unusually long) ship. If the speaker points to the bow of the ship through window A and says, 'That ship is an aircraft carrier', the hearer does not understand what the speaker is saying if he takes her to be talking of the ship whose stern they can see through window B. Yet it is the same ship, so the thoughts 'That $ship_{bow}$ is an aircraft carrier', and 'That $ship_{stern}$ is an aircraft carrier' have the same singular truth-conditions (they are both true if and only if the ship—the same in both cases—is an aircraft carrier). Here again it follows that the mode of presentation (the way the ship is thought about) is essential to what is communicated.

[7] Analogous examples can be found in Textor (2015) and Garcia-Carpintero (2016).

merely the communication of truth-conditional content. Some suitable relation (weaker than identity but stronger than mere coreferentiality) has got to hold between the modes of presentation respectively deployed by the speaker and the hearer in successful indexical communication. The problem of characterizing that relation is similar to the problem of *cognitive dynamics*—the problem of specifying the relation that must hold between the modes of presentation deployed by a single individual at different times t and t' for the subject to count as having 'retained', at t', the temporally indexical belief held at t (e.g. the belief that it is 1:00 p.m.).[8]

7.2. *Indexical Communication in the Mental File Framework*

So what *is* wrong with the Naïve Conception? Among the diagnostics which have been offered, some aim to *protect* the Naïve Conception from the indexical counterexamples. Thus it is common to hold that what is communicated, and therefore replicated, is not the speaker's indexical thought (which cannot be shared) but an *ersatz* thought, a substitute or 'surrogate'. This solution has attracted attention lately (Torre 2010, Moss 2012, Kölbel 2013). It was originally put forward by Frege in a well-known and somewhat mysterious passage:

Every one is presented to himself in a particular and primitive way, in which he is presented to no one else. So, when Dr. Lauben thinks that he has been wounded, he will probably take as a basis this primitive way in which he is presented to himself. And only Dr. Lauben himself can grasp thoughts determined in this way. But now he may want to communicate with others. He cannot communicate a thought which he alone can grasp. Therefore, if he now says 'I have been wounded', he must use the 'I' in a

---

[8] On the problem of cognitive dynamics, see Chapter 5.

sense which can be grasped by others, perhaps in the sense of 'he who is speaking to you at this moment'. (Frege 1967b: 25–6)

What Frege suggests in that passage is that the thought communicated is not the speaker's (incommunicable) first-person thought but another, suitably related thought. There is replication, on that view, but what is replicated is not the speaker's first-person thought.

Does the 'substitution' strategy make it possible to rescue the Naïve Conception? I do not think so. The Naïve Conception comports two tenets, which Weber calls the 'mind-to-speech principle' and the 'speech-to-mind principle' (Weber 2013: S208):

(Mind to speech)   *Speaker's thought = thought expressed by the utterance.*

(Speech to mind)   *Thought expressed by the utterance = hearer's thought.*

Frege's suggestion sacrifices the first tenet of the view. He takes the thought expressed by a first-person utterance (its semantic content) to be distinct from the speaker's incommunicable first-person thought. Other authors are willing to sacrifice the other tenet. Thus Dummett (1981: 122) says that in communication, it is sufficient for the hearer to *recognize* the thought expressed by the utterance (which, for Dummett, *is* the speaker's thought). The hearer recognizes the speaker's thought, but that thought does not become the hearer's thought—it remains bound to the speaker.[9]

---

[9] On Dummett's view, it is unnecessary to distinguish between the thought which Lauben privately entertains and the thought he communicates. One may, instead, distinguish between *thinking* a thought and *grasping* it. The hearer can grasp the thought an utterance expresses (i.e. know which thought is expressed), even if she cannot think it. 'Although you, the hearer, know what thought I had when I thought to myself, "I have been wounded", you cannot think that thought yourself. What this shows is that Frege was wrong to say, as he did, that to think is to grasp thoughts, at least if grasping a thought is the same as knowing what thought it is. Hence, even if there are thoughts which only one person can think, or which only a person in some given situation can think, there is no need to conclude that there are thoughts that cannot be communicated' (Dummett 1981: 122).

Gibbard (2012) and Weber (2013) say that the hearer's thought is not identical to the thought expressed by the utterance (which, for them also, is the speaker's thought): it results from a *Transform-and-Recentre* operation on it. In a similar vein, Kölbel (2013) distinguishes the semantic content of a sentence (what it expresses in context) from its 'conversational content' which is communicated to the hearer.[10]

In earlier work (Recanati 1993, 1995, 2012) I presented another interpretation of Frege's passage, based on my own distinction between linguistic and psychological modes of presentation (Recanati 1990). I don't claim that that interpretation corresponds to what Frege actually meant, only that this view, inspired by Frege's passage, provides an interesting solution to the problem of indexical communication—a solution which, in the Appendix, I compare to the other solutions currently on the market.

Linguistic modes of presentation are whatever information is linguistically encoded about the reference. 'I' encodes the information that the referent is the speaker, 'you' that it is the hearer, and so on and so forth. Psychological modes of presentation are the ways the subject *thinks* of the reference. When the speaker says 'I', she thinks of herself in the first-person way, but the hearer who understands her thinks of her in a different way. The interpersonal variability of psychological modes of presentation establishes that linguistic and psychological modes of presentation are distinct, for the linguistic mode of presentation is constant: 'I' means the same thing for the speaker and the hearer. The same conclusion can be reached by considering demonstratives: it is possible for a rational subject to think 'That is F but that is not F', even if the two occurrences of 'that' refer to the same object. In such a case, one has to posit two distinct (psychological) modes of presentation to satisfy the basic constraint which governs them: the so-called 'Frege's Constraint' (Section 1.3). But there is a single linguistic mode of presentation associated with 'that': a single piece of

---

[10] See the Appendix for detailed discussion of these views.

linguistic knowledge about the referent is encoded in the word. Again we reach the conclusion that linguistic and psychological modes of presentation are different.[11]

Psychological modes of presentation, in my framework, are mental files. The SELF file is based on a special ER relation, a relation one bears to oneself and to no one else. (That relation is identity.) The speaker who thinks about himself in the first-person way deploys such a file. The file stores information the speaker gains about himself in the first-person way. Since the speaker is aware of being the speaker, the piece of information encoded by the word 'I' (the property of being the speaker) corresponds to a piece of information *in* the file. The hearer also has a file about the speaker, and that file also contains that piece of information (since the hearer is witnessing the speech event and knows that the speaker is speaking to him). So the linguistic mode of presentation corresponds to a piece of information that is common to both the speaker's and the hearer's files about the speaker. These files are distinct, and they are of different types, but they are constrained by the linguistic mode of presentation. The linguistic constraint on files is a means for coordinating them.[12]

---

[11] A further argument for the distinction between linguistic and psychological modes of presentation involves the sort of example I discussed in Section 1.2: 'I met my new neighbour$_i$ the other day. The bastard$_i$ did not greet me.' Here as elsewhere in this book coindexing marks coreference *de jure*. Anyone who wonders whether or not 'my new neighbour' and 'the bastard' corefer is someone who has not (yet) understood the utterance. Now, as we have seen, (strong) coreference *de jure* correlates with sameness of mode of presentation. So we want the two descriptions—'my new neighbour' and 'the bastard'—to be associated with the same mode of presentation, even though the linguistic modes of presentation associated with these descriptions are different: the referent is presented as the speaker's new neighbour in one case, and as a bastard in the other case. It follows that there must be modes of presentation in the psychological sense, distinct from the linguistic modes of presentation.

[12] In addition to the constraints that are linguistically encoded (e.g. the constraint that the referent be the speaker, in the case of 'I'), there are constraints that are contextually conveyed. In Loar's example, discussed in Section 7.1, the referent is linguistically constrained to be a male person (for the speaker refers to him as 'he') and contextually constrained to be the man being interviewed on television (for the speaker is looking at him while speaking). Coordination fails because the hearer misidentifies the contextual constraint and, as a result, activates the wrong file (which turns out to be about the same individual). In 'From Coordination to Content'

On this interpretation the linguistic modes of presentation are not *ersatz* ingredients of thought. They are not thought constituents, but they are suitably related to the relevant thought constituents. The thought constituents are the files—the psychological modes of presentation—which the linguistic modes of presentation constrain. It follows that communication involves, not replication, but coordination of thoughts. The coordination aspect is obvious in cases of joint attention accompanying the use of demonstratives. The speaker and the hearer do not have the same perspective on the object of attention but their attentional acts are coordinated and converge on the object. Similarly, the mental acts of reference performed by the speaker and the hearer by means of their respective files about the speaker are coordinated through, *inter alia*, the linguistic mode of presentation encoded by the word 'I'.

Which of the two tenets of the Naïve Conception am I rejecting? I am rejecting both. The two tenets appeal to the notion of 'the thought expressed by the utterance'. Let us call the thesis that there is such a thing the *presupposition* of the Naïve Conception. Since the speaker's thought and the hearer's thought are different, the presupposition creates a problem. To solve it, we have to equate the thought expressed by the utterance *either* with the speaker's thought or with the hearer's thought (unless we can think of yet another candidate). But this creates another problem:

One possible objection to this move is that it is somehow arbitrary. How do we choose the particular point of view to be privileged? On intuitive grounds it seems natural to select the point of view of the speaker, yet there are *also* reasons to select the hearer's point of view. As Evans emphasized, what matters, when we want to individuate semantic content, is what would count as a proper *understanding* of an utterance (Evans 1982: 92, 143n, 171, etc.); but 'understanding' defines the task of the hearer.   (Recanati 1995: 98)

(2013), Cumming adds a further constraint of one-to-one match between the files respectively deployed by the speaker and the hearer.

To escape the charge of arbitrariness, the solution I recommend is to *give up the presupposition of the Naïve Conception* (hence its two tenets, since they both rest on it). We have to give up the very notion of '*the* thought expressed by the utterance'. There is no such thing: there is the speaker's thought and the thought formed by the hearer if communication is successful (Bezuidenhout 1997). That is all there is as far as thoughts are concerned. We don't need an additional entity, the thought expressed by the utterance.[13]

7.3. Conclusion

Mental indexicality exists, and to make sense of it we must revert to the ancient conception of thought which Hintikka advertises (Section 7.1), and which so much impressed Prior when he read about it in Geach's review of Mates's *Stoic Logic* (Mates 1953, Geach 1955, Prior 1967: 15–16). The conception has recently become popular, thanks to the work of philosophers such as David Lewis. Following Lewis, the content of an indexical thought can be modelled as a set of centred worlds—a centred content. To avoid Lewis's partial descriptivism, one can make the content multi-centred, as Ninan (2013) has suggested. But it is essential to make room for another level of content in addition to the centred content. An indexical thought, construed as involving mental assent (so: the *assertion* of a centred content), determines objective truth-conditions. These truth-conditions are the level of content we need to make sense of interpersonal disagreement or intrapersonal change of mind.

The two-level conception I advocate is in many ways similar to Stalnaker's recent theory of 'belief states' (comprised of a base

[13] Heck comes to the same conclusion, on very much the same grounds (Heck 2002: 42–3).

world and a set of centred worlds). The view I advocate, however, is a variant of Perry's approach, which Stalnaker has criticized. Like Perry, I appeal to vehicles (mental files) and modes of presentation (the 'import' of the files). Stalnaker thinks this blurs the line between representations and their contents, but I have argued that the criticism is misplaced (Section 6.2). Stalnaker himself says that we need to connect the world as the subject takes it to be with the subject himself and the world as it is: that is the key to his notion of a belief state. Now I hold that the vehicles (the mental files) are a crucial aspect of the 'base world' (the world as it is, centred on the subject). They provide an essential connection to 'the world as the subject takes it to be'. The files which the subject deploys in the base world determine the individuals which exist in the centred worlds representing the subject's doxastic alternatives. The presuppositions embodied in the system of mental representations deployed by the subject provide the *structure* of her belief world (at a time).

The information conveyed by an utterance has to be integrated into that pre-existing structure.[14] Understanding a referring expression involves deploying a mental file, and thereby (hopefully) mentally referring to some object via the ER relation on which the file is based. The mental file to be deployed is constrained by the linguistic meaning of the referring expression (the linguistic mode of presentation). In this framework, the communication problem is solved: one gives up the Naïve Conception of Communication as the replication of thoughts, in favour of a conception on which the speaker's and the hearer's thoughts are merely coordinated (via the constraints on files, both linguistic and contextual, which apply equally to all the speech participants). One gives up even the most basic presupposition of the Naïve Conception: that there is such a thing as 'the' thought expressed by an utterance.

---

[14] Sometimes, linguistic information leads to *restructuring*, as when one learns an identity (Lockwood 1971, Strawson 1974: 54–6).

8

Dynamic Files in Communication

8.1. Interpersonal Dynamic Files

Through the linguistic meaning of an indexical (and further constraints provided by context) the speaker and the hearer coordinate their files about the reference. In some cases the difference between their respective files—corresponding to a difference in their ER relations to the reference—manifests itself as a difference in the words they use to corefer. The speaker says 'I', the hearer responds by saying 'you', as in the following dialogue:

LAUBEN: 'I have been wounded.'

LEO PETER: 'You have been wounded, really?'

The indexicals used by Lauben ('I') and Leo Peter ('you') are not merely coreferential: they are coreferential *de jure* (Prosser forthcoming). Leo Peter takes it for granted that the person talking to him (and self-ascribing the property of having been wounded) is the person he is now addressing in his response. Lauben likewise takes it for granted that the person Leo Peter is addressing is himself. These 'discourse-internal identities' are presupposed (Perry 1980a, Spencer 2006). Since Lauben and Leo Peter both unreflectively assume that Leo Peter's use of 'you' corefers with Lauben's use of 'I', they engage in what Prosser calls 'transparent communication', based on a shared presupposition of coreference. *But the presupposition may be false*: the person Leo Peter addresses when he says 'You have been wounded, really?' may not be the person who actually said 'I have been wounded'.

Imagine that Leo Peter actually misheard Lauben's utterance as coming from the mouth of Elwood Fritchley, and uttered 'You have been wounded, really?' *in addressing Fritchley*. (To flesh out the example, imagine also that Lauben did not notice, and thought Leo Peter was addressing him.) In such a case of confusion, Peter's use of 'you' fails to refer because it simultaneously tracks two distinct persons: the person who said 'I have been wounded' (Lauben) and the person Peter is addressing (Elwood Fritchley). But, even in that situation, Lauben's use of 'I' straightforwardly refers: it refers to the reference of the SELF file which Lauben associates with his use of 'I' (namely, himself). Lauben's SELF file is not confused, contrary to the file deployed by Leo Peter when he says 'you'. This is a case of 'type 3' (Section 2.4), structurally similar to the Zach–Wally case: one term refers, the other one fails to refer.[1]

As we saw in discussing the Zach–Wally example, we can take either an intrapersonal or an interpersonal perspective on such cases. From an intrapersonal perspective, Zach associates the same confused file with Wally's use of 'he' and with his own use of 'he'; that is because he misinterprets Wally's use (not understanding it refers to Udo). The two file deployments occasioned by the conversation *in Zach's mind* are coreferential *de jure* in the strong sense: they are synchronous deployments of the same file. But from an *interpersonal* point of view, the situation is different. Wally's use of 'he' refers to Udo, while Zach's use of 'he' fails to refer. Zach's file is confused, but Wally's file is not. Similarly, in the

---

[1] The Zach–Wally case: *Wally says of Udo, 'He needs a haircut', and Zach, thinking to agree, but looking at another person, says, 'he sure does'* (Lawlor 2010: 4).

example we imagined, Lauben straightforwardly refers to himself by deploying his SELF file, while Leo Peter in his response deploys a confused file which fails to refer. The fact that such cases are possible shows that the relation of coreference *de jure* which holds interpersonally and underlies transparent communication in Prosser's sense is weak CDJ.[2]

In Chapter 5 I introduced the notion of a *dynamic file*: a sequence of file-stages bound together by the relation of (weak) coreference *de jure*. The notion was applied to diachronic deployments of files, but it applies to interpersonal deployments as well (see Prosser forthcoming). In a conversation in which the speaker says 'I' and the hearer *de jure* corefers by saying 'you', the coordinated files deployed by the speaker and the hearer constitute a sequence: an interpersonal dynamic file. Like dynamic files in general, such sequences only support weak CDJ, because the presuppositions which make trading on identity possible may turn out to be false.

8.2. *Interpersonal Recurrence: Sharing a Language*

As Prosser emphasizes, use of *the same word* by the interlocutors typically triggers a presupposition of coreference. In a conversation in which different tokens of a given word are produced by the speech participants, the tokens are *de jure* coreferential (unless something defeats the presupposition). It is presupposed that all the users use the word in the same way:[3]

---

[2] In the last section of his paper, Prosser himself notes that the coreference *de jure* relation that underlies transparent communication is not transitive.

[3] See Section 1.1, where this point has already been made (following Taylor and Fiengo and May). See also Schroeter: 'When you hear someone use the term "water" in a normal English sentence, you naturally presume that the other person must be referring to the very same kind of stuff that you yourself pick out with that term' (2012: 2).

I propose [. . .] that two individuals think of an object under the same [dynamic] mode of presentation just when their thoughts are epistemically related to one another in such a way that they can trade on identity of reference. *This occurs whenever there is a shared word the co-reference of whose tokens is taken for granted.* This includes, but is not limited to, cases in which one speaker defers to another. Modes of presentation can be shared by members of the same linguistic community who have never actually spoken to one another, provided they would recognise each other's utterances as containing a shared word were they to speak.   (Prosser forthcoming: 12, emphasis mine)

On this view, just in virtue of using the same word, the conversational protagonists coordinate their files about the reference. They 'bootstrap their way to same-saying', as Laura Schroeter (2012) puts it. The files thus coordinated constitute an interpersonal dynamic file (a mode of presentation in Prosser's dynamic sense).

The notion of an interpersonal dynamic file based on recurrence of the same word (presupposed to carry the same semantic value) is reminiscent of that of a *communicative chain* which has been at the forefront of attention in the philosophical literature on proper names (Geach 1969, Kripke 1980, Evans 1973, Devitt 1981, 2015, Dickie 2015, Kamp 2015).[4] According to Kripke, when a speaker is introduced to a name through a use of it by another speaker, and starts using the name on his own, the presupposition that he thereby corefers with the first speaker becomes operative, and a reference chain is created. Devitt characterizes what he calls a d-chain ('designating chain') as follows:

A name token designates an object if and only if underlying the name is a d[esignating]-chain grounded in the object. D[esignating]-chains consist of three different kinds of link: groundings which link the chain to an object,

---

⁴ There is a parallel literature on so-called anaphoric chains. See e.g. Chastain 1975, Sommers 1982, Burge 1983, Berger 2002, and the vast literature on dynamic semantics stemming from Karttunen 1976.

abilities to designate, and communication situations in which abilities are passed on or reinforced (reference borrowings).   (1981: 64)

Reference chains branch, and when they do the notion of a 'chain' becomes somewhat inappropriate. A language user is typically exposed to uses of the name belonging to several branches of the same 'chain' (and possibly to several chains grounded in the same object). Each exposition reinforces her ability to designate by using the name. As Devitt notes:

Underlying a person's use of a name may be many designating-chains involving multiple reference-borrowings and, ultimately, multiple groundings in the object: there may be a *causal network* of designating-chains underlying her use.   (Devitt 2015: 117)

Across the network, every use is presupposed to carry the same reference as the other uses.

Mental files come into play in this case as it does in the case of indexicals. Each individual user associates the name with a mental file about the reference of the name. So, corresponding to the network of uses, there is what Perry calls an 'intersubjective file network' (Perry 2012b: 200–4), constituted by the files associated with the name by the users in the network. (Kamp 2015: 309 calls it an 'intersubjective causal network of entity representations'). Perry emphasizes the relation of 'coco-reference' (weak coreference *de jure*) which ties together the files in the network.

So far, names and indexicals have been described in similar ways: both are associated with mental files in communication, and the mental files they are associated with in the mind of the conversational protagonists coordinate and give rise to interpersonal dynamic files. But there is an important difference. Proper names, I will now argue, are associated with a special kind of dynamic file: a distributed file. Such a file exists in a stable manner in the community of language users, in contrast to the dynamic files associated with the use of indexicals.

8.3. *Distributed Files*

Recall Taylor's view that proper names are *essentially* devices of coreference (Section 1.1). This idea can be cashed out as follows. The role of names is to coordinate the mental files of all of those who are involved in the name-using practice (which goes well beyond the local contexts of indexical communication). Through a name, the linguistic community *interconnects* the individual files in the minds of name users, thus making information transfer between the files possible through testimony and chains of communication using the name. Kamp speaks of 'the causal coordination of labelled entity representations that are privy to the members of the community' (Kamp 2015: 298). The files thus interconnected can be viewed as a global, *distributed file* in which the community pools information about the referent.

A reader for Oxford University Press objected to the pooling idea, on the grounds that the information in the files of individual language users does not automatically become available to the other language users ('I can keep a secret'). But the pooling idea should be understood in the light of Putnam's 'division of linguistic labor' (Putnam 1975: 227–9). The reference of a name (or rather, its 'denotation'—see Section 8.4) is *fixed at the community level*, as we shall see: it is the reference of the distributed file. The distributed file itself shouldn't be seen as the static juxtaposition of individual mental files, but as a *public file* managed by the community as a whole. The community filters out information tentatively contributed to the distributed file by screening testimony and correcting tentative individual contributions when they do not fit.[5] In this way the community pools information from the interconnected

---

[5] For example, if I tell you that Napoleon died a few years ago, you will act as a gatekeeper and do your best to prevent that piece of alleged testimony from entering the public file associated with the name 'Napoleon'.

individual files so as to build a coherent body of information about the reference of the distributed file.

What fixes the reference of the distributed file is what Devitt calls the process of 'grounding'. Grounding always proceeds through individual mental files in the minds of the language users. The reference of the distributed file is a function of the references of all the (non-parasitic) individual mental files associated with the name by its users, and more precisely of all the partial references determined by the ER relations on which individual files are based. Mental files refer through ER relations, and by their reference contribute to determining the reference of the distributed file to which they belong. So distributed files are multiply grounded.

Devitt rightly criticizes those who hold that grounding occurs only in the beginning, when a referential chain starts its life:

What is it [. . .] that grounds the name in a certain object? It is the causal-perceptual link between the first users of the name and the object named. What made it the case that this particular object got named in such a situation was its unique place in the causal nexus in the grounding situation.

It is important to note that this sort of situation will typically arise many times in the history of an object after it has been initially named: names are typically *multiply grounded* in their bearers. These other situations are ones where the name is used as a result of a direct perceptual confrontation with its bearer.   (Devitt 2015: 114)

Devitt acknowledges that there are other sorts of groundings than direct perceptual grounding (he talks of 'indirect grounding'). All things considered, it is all the uses of a name, save for its purely deferential (parasitic) uses, which contribute to grounding the name. Such multiple grounding is what explains reference change. A significant change in the pattern of groundings (as when 'Madagascar'-users started to massively associate individual mental files about the island with the name) can determine a shift in the reference of the name.

Distributed files, I said, are public files managed by the community as a whole.[6] Each user is responsible for grounding, via his/her file based on various ER relations, the distributed file of the community, but it is up to the community to purge the file from inconsistencies, by correcting individual uses when necessary, so as to maintain a coherent pool of distributed information.

When a name is used purely deferentially (as when one picks up a name overheard in a conversation), the individual mental file the language user associates with the name is a *deferential file*: a file based on a specific ER relation, that of being party to a proper name-using practice (Recanati 1997b, 2000, 2001). Being party to a proper name-using practice (through acquiring the name from someone else) is an epistemically rewarding relation: one is in a position to gain information about the referent of the name through testimony (by attending to the name when it is used, or by using it oneself to elicit information from others). One has access to the distributed file of the community. Let us call that ER relation, made available by the mere sharing of words, the 'deferential relation'. The deferential relation 'broaden[s] the horizons of thought', as Kaplan puts it (Kaplan 1989b: 603). It makes it possible to think and talk about objects and properties one is not acquainted with:

My dog, being color-blind, cannot entertain the thought that I am wearing a red shirt. But my color-blind colleague can entertain even the thought that *Aristotle* wore a red shirt.   (Kaplan 1989b: 604)

However, a deferential file, based on the deferential relation (and no other ER relation), is only a *stage* in the development of a full-fledged encyclopedia entry based on as many ER relations as happen to be available in context (Section 5.3). The additional ER

---

[6] In Recanati 2012: 204–5, I suggest that public files can be used to make sense of Geach's Hob-Nob example (Geach 1967). The two individual files in the mind of Hob and Nob are coreferential *de jure* despite the lack of direct communication between them because they are part of a network managed as a distributed file.

relations on which individual encyclopedia entries are normally based contribute to grounding the communal name and the distributed file associated with it.

From what I have said, it follows that the individual files and the distributed file are referentially interdependent (in a non-circular manner). The reference of the individual encyclopedia entry in the user's mind depends, *inter alia*, upon the deferential relation established via the name and the distributed file associated with it. If the individual file is based *only* on that deferential relation (as in the case of deferential files), it does not contribute to grounding but inherits the reference of the distributed file, thereby making it possible for a language user with no knowledge of an object to refer to it both in speech and thought. Such a parasitic use takes advantage of the fact that the reference of a name (what I am about to call its 'denotation') is fixed by the distributed file. In the other direction, however, the reference of the distributed file itself depends on the references of the individual files in the network (unless they are purely deferential files).

8.4. *Reference and Denotation*

When a name is used, there are two files to consider: the individual encyclopedia entry in the mind of the name user and the distributed file, i.e. the network of which the individual file is a node. The individual encyclopedia entry refers through all the ER relations it is based on (including the relation of being party to the name-using practice). Let us assume that an encyclopedia entry refers to the 'dominant source of information' in the file (Evans 1973, Recanati 2012: 140). It does not matter how exactly we cash out the vague notion of 'dominant source of information'.[7] What matters is that

---

[7] See Dickie 2015 (chapter 5) for an improvement over Evans's account.

the dominant source of information in the individual file need not be the same thing as the reference of the distributed file.

The reference of the individual file and that of the distributed file are interdependent, but they can diverge. The reference of the distributed file and that of the individual file diverge in all cases in which (i) the deferential ER relation which contributes to determining the reference of the individual file and makes it dependent upon the reference of the distributed file counts as less important in context than some more direct, e.g. perceptual, relation to the reference, and (ii) the more direct relation targets an object which turns out to be distinct from the reference of the distributed file. This situation is illustrated by Kripke's famous example:

Two people see Smith in a distance and mistake him for Jones. They have a brief colloquy: 'What is Jones doing?' 'Raking the leaves.' 'Jones', in the common language of both, is a name of Jones; it *never* names Smith. Yet, in some sense, on this occasion, clearly both participants in the dialogue have referred to Smith.   (Kripke 1977: 263)

The individual files in the mind of the language users in this example are confused files partly referring to Smith and partly to Jones (Devitt 2015: 118–21). But the distributed file associated with the name 'Jones' unambiguously refers to Jones. The particular mistake made by these particular users hardly affects the reference of the distributed file.

When there is referential divergence between the distributed file and the individual file associated with the name by a particular user of the name, the use of the name is deemed *incorrect* by the community (as part of its corrective policy with respect to distributed files). In Kripke's example, the use of the name 'Jones' will be judged incorrect by any member of the community apprised of the fact that the man raking the leaves is *not* Jones. The two users themselves, when apprised of the facts, will recognize that their use is incorrect. This strongly suggests that the reference of the name is the reference of the distributed file, rather than the reference of the individual encylopedia entry.

But if the reference of a name is the reference of the distributed file rather than the reference of the individual file in the mind of the name user, this is a noticeable exception to the principle that the reference of a referring expression is the reference of the file associated with it in the mind of the expression's user. We have to concede that, sometimes, the principle fails. When a proper name is used, the reference of the file in the mind of the name user is the 'speaker's reference', but that does not necessarily coincide with the *semantic reference* of the name (Kripke 1977).

But one may resist the concession, and the general idea that there is 'semantic reference' over and above the reference determined by the files in the minds of the language users. According to philosophers of a contextualist persuasion, from Peter Strawson to Donnellan to Stephen Neale, there is *only* speaker's reference. Referring is not something expressions do. Proper names do not refer, only uses of proper names do (and a 'use' of a proper name necessarily involves the deployment of a file). We can still make sense of the contrast between semantic reference and speaker's reference, however (Recanati 2018); but we have to reinterpret it.

In the case of definite descriptions, Donnellan distinguishes the *denotation* (i.e. the unique object which satisfies the matrix of the description) and the *reference* (what the subject 'has in mind'—the reference of the mental file he or she deploys while uttering the description). An attributive description denotes, Donnellan says, but it does not refer (since there is no object the speaker has in mind).[8] If the description is used referentially, the speaker deploys

---

[8] 'Whether or not a description is used referentially [. . .], it may have a denotation. Hence, denoting and referring, as I have explicated the latter notion, are distinct . . . If one tried to maintain that they are the same notion, one result would be that a speaker might be referring to something without knowing it. If someone said, for example, in 1960, before he had any idea that Mr Goldwater would be the Republican nominee in 1964, "The Republican candidate for president in 1964 will be a conservative," (perhaps on the basis of an analysis of the views of party leaders) the definite description here would *denote* Mr Goldwater. But would we wish to say

a mental file and refers to some object, which may or may not satisfy the description. If the object referred to satisfies the description, it counts as 'semantic reference' on the new interpretation of that notion (Recanati 2018). If it doesn't, it counts as mere 'speaker's reference'. On this view, in contrast to Kripke's, there are two orthogonal distinctions: between denotation and (speaker's) reference, and between two kinds of (speaker's) reference: semantic reference and 'mere' speaker's reference.

We can apply this theory to proper names. Let us first distinguish between proper nouns and proper names:

Names vs nouns

Proper nouns are vocabulary items. Different homonymous names (such as 'Aristotle', which is both the name of the Ancient philosopher and the given name of Onassis) are made up of the same proper noun. In contrast to the noun, the name is associated with a particular individual, known as its 'bearer'. That is why there are two distinct names 'Aristotle', each associated with a distinct bearer, while there is a single noun 'Aristotle', which is assigned to both the philosopher and the shipping magnate.

Next, let us distinguish between a name and a use of that name:

Names vs uses of names

In using a name, the speaker deploys a mental file, whereby (if all goes well) he or she refers to a definite individual. Although it has a bearer, the name itself does not 'refer' in Donnellan's sense. By analogy with Donnellan's treatment of definite descriptions, we may call the bearer of a name its *denotation*. Names denote, while uses of names refer.

that the speaker had referred to, mentioned, or talked about Mr Goldwater? I feel these terms would be out of place' (Donnellan 1966, in Schwartz: 54–5).

Now we are in a position to reinstate the semantic reference/ speaker's reference distinction as a distinction internal to reference as opposed to denotation (just as we did for definite descriptions).

In the current framework, the denotation of a name is determined by the pattern of groundings characteristic of the distributed file. Since the groundings take place via the individual mental files in the minds of users of the name, the denotation of a name is a function of what the individual files which make up the distributed file (partially) refer to. Still, the denotation of a name is distinct from the reference of a particular use of the name. A use of a name refers via the mental file deployed by the speaker. By using the name, the speaker presupposes that the individual he or she is referring to is the bearer of the name (the denotation). Here, as in the case of definite descriptions, there are two options: either the presupposition is satisfied or it is not. If it is, the reference counts as semantic reference. If it is not, then, to the extent that the speaker succeeds in (confusedly) referring to the object she has in mind, this counts as mere speaker's reference. Both cases are compatible with the principle that the reference of an expression always is the reference of a file in the mind of the expression's user.

Appendix to Part II

Communication with Centred Contents: A Survey

A.1. *The Lewisian Dilemma: Egan*

INTEREST in the problem of indexical communication has recently been fuelled by the success of Lewis's centred worlds approach to mental indexicality.[1] According to Lewis, the subject who thinks an indexical thought (or any thought, for that matter) self-ascribes a property, which can be modelled as a set of centred worlds. Hume and Heimson both self-ascribe the property of being Hume, and having written the *Treatise*. Lewis's approach was acclaimed as requiring only minimal amendment to the possible worlds framework used in semantic approaches to the attitudes: one only has to take the possible worlds representing the subject's doxastic alternatives to be 'centred' on an individual at a time to capture what is distinctive of indexical thought—its perspectival character. But Stalnaker objected that this fine-grained approach to content

makes it more difficult to compare past with present beliefs, and, more important, to explain the relations between the beliefs of different persons—relations that are essential to a natural explanation of the exchange of information. (Stalnaker 1981: 146)

Imagine a subject who, on Monday, thinks 'Today is Mary's birthday', and retains that belief until the next day. The next day, if he has kept track of time, he will think 'Yesterday was Mary's birthday'. The belief has been retained, so there must be a certain content that is the content of the belief that is retained. But the sets of centred worlds by means of which Lewis represents the content of the indexical beliefs respectively held on

---

[1] Credit for the approach should be given also to Chisholm, who argued for it independently of Lewis. See the citations and references in Recanati 2007: 17n.

Monday and Tuesday are different sets. Or suppose the amnesiac Lingens meets Ortcutt in the Stanford Library and asks him: 'Who am I?' Ortcutt answers: 'You are Lingens'. It seems that Ortcutt provides the requested information as directly and explicitly as possible, but that is not what the centred worlds model says. According to the model:

Lingens asks which of a certain set of properties is correctly ascribed to himself. Ortcutt responds by ascribing a *different* property to *himself*. Lingens is then able to infer the answer to his question from Ortcutt's assertion. (Stalnaker 1981: 147)

Stalnaker finds this too complicated[2] and suggests looking for an ordinary possible worlds proposition to be the communicated content, shared by the interlocutors (or the content of the belief that is retained in the Monday/Tuesday case); he therefore suggests giving up Lewis's theory instead of giving up the Naïve Conception of Communication, according to which the communicated content must be shared by the interlocutors.[3]

In the past few years, several philosophers have tried to *reconcile* Lewis's framework with the Naïve Conception of Communication endorsed by Stalnaker. The first attempt was made by Andy Egan in 'Epistemic Modals, Relativism and Assertion' (2007). Egan assumes the Naïve Conception, which he finds 'pretty plausible', while acknowledging

---

[2] Not everyone does. Gibbard analyses a standard episode of communication as follows: 'Speaker Ann expresses something of how things are from her own standpoint. Ben the hearer, knowing how things are from Ann's standpoint, draws on whatever he knows about her standpoint in relation to his own, and uses this to conclude something of how things are from his own standpoint' (Gibbard 2012: 260). Likewise Weber (2013: S222): 'As the speaker doesn't merely characterize the world she shares with the hearer, but rather represents something about her individual location within it, the hearer cannot directly endorse the information expressed. She gains information about her own location from information about a different location and her beliefs about how she is related to that location'. (For more about Gibbard's and Weber's view, see the last three sections of this Appendix.)

[3] In more recent work (2008, 2014), Stalnaker has come to appreciate the usefulness of centred contents for representing the internal aspect of content (the subject's doxastic alternatives); but he 'links' the centred worlds in the internal content to the subject and the time in the 'base world', thereby simultaneously providing the external component (hence the possible worlds truth-conditions) and capturing the fact that indexical thoughts are 'context-bound'. As noted already, Stalnaker's approach is similar to the two-levels-of content approach I defend in Recanati (2007).

that it leads to disaster when applied to the communication of centred contents. Egan summarizes the Naïve Conception as follows:

In ordinary cases of successful assertion, there is a single proposition P which is (a) believed by the person making the assertion, (b) the content of the utterance used to make the assertion, and (c) comes to be believed, as a result of the assertion, by the other parties to the conversation.   (Egan 2007: 12)

The Naïve Conception leads to disaster if we further assume that 'My pants are on fire' expresses a centred content, namely a set of worlds centred on a person whose pants are on fire. For the Naïve Conception entails that the trusting hearer will accept the content expressed by the speaker, hence, in this case, self-ascribe the property of having one's pants on fire. But of course, in real life the trusting hearer to whom the speaker says 'My pants are on fire' will not form the belief that his own pants are on fire! Egan notes, however, that the Naïve Conception has disastrous consequences, when applied to the communication of centred content, only if the speaker's and the interlocutor's contexts are relevantly dissimilar. If the contexts are relevantly similar (e.g. the speaker and the hearer are in the same place at the same time and the speaker says 'Sydney is near'), then both the speaker and his addressee will unproblematically self-ascribe the property that is the (centred) content of the utterance (the property of being near Sydney): the Naïve Conception no longer has disastrous consequences, in such a setting. It would have disastrous consequences only if the hearer was located in a different place than the speaker, far from Sydney. The utterance by the speaker of the sentence, 'Sydney is near', which expresses his thought would be *illegitimate* in such a setting. It follows that the tension between the centred worlds framework and the Naïve Conception of Communication can be alleviated by suitably *restricting* the use of centred contents in communication.

According to Egan, the following is an inconsistent triad, given the belief-transfer model of assertion which he takes from Stalnaker (1978):

(1)   The utterance expresses a centred content.

(2)   The hearer is in a relevantly dissimilar context.

(3)   Communication proceeds smoothly.

If (1) and (2) are true, (3) must be false: communication fails when the utterance expresses a centred content which is not 'locally portable' and cannot be shared by the hearer.[4] If (1) and (3) are true, (2) must be false: if the content is *de se* yet communication proceeds smoothly, the hearer must be in a relevantly similar context. If (2) and (3) are true, (1) must be false: if the contexts are dissimilar yet communication proceeds smoothly, that means that what the utterance expresses is not a centred content.

A consequence of the theory is that 'My pants are on fire' does *not* express a centred content. This follows from the fact that, when Kaplan utters that sentence to his sister, communication proceeds smoothly even though the contexts are relevantly dissimilar: (2) and (3) are true, so (1) must be false. Egan accepts that, and concludes that 'My pants are on fire' expresses an ordinary possible worlds proposition (true if and only if Kaplan's pants are on fire) rather than a centred content. As he puts it (Egan 2007: 12): 'If we're going to accept the belief-transfer model of assertion, we had better reject the semantic theory that says that utterances of "My pants are on fire" express PANTS' ('PANTS' is Egan's name for the centred proposition that one's pants are on fire). Still, 'Sydney is near', or 'Bond might be in Zurich', do express centred contents, in Egan's framework. The Naïve Conception (and its potentially disastrous consequences when applied to the communication of *de se* content) provides Egan with a criterion for deciding *when* an utterance expresses a centred content and when it does not.

Has Egan managed to reconcile Lewis's centred worlds approach with the Naïve Conception of Communication? He hasn't. The state of mind of the speaker who suddenly realizes what's happening and exclaims, 'My pants are on fire!' (and acts accordingly) is one of the things Lewis's theory of centred content is meant to capture. The subject self-ascribes the property $\lambda x.x$'s *pants are on fire*. That's what is common to all of those who think their pants are on fire and act accordingly. But for Egan, that relativized proposition is *not* the content of the utterance: the content of the utterance cannot be centred in that way, if the Naïve Conception of

---

[4] A content is *portable*, according to Kölbel (2013: 100–2), if its truth-value is perspective-invariant, and *portable relative to a given class of perspectives* iff its truth-value is invariant across perspectives within the class. A content is *locally portable* (in a conversation) iff the perspectives of the conversationalists belong to a class relative to which the content of the utterance is portable. A content must at least be locally portable if it is to be shared by the conversational participants.

Communication is correct, because if it were all the parties to the conversation would have to self-ascribe the property as well. So Egan faces a dilemma. Either he has to give up Lewis's analysis of first-person thoughts (by denying that such thoughts are centred), or he has to deny that the speaker's first-person *utterance* expresses his centred *thought*.[5] Egan is likely to choose the latter option (insofar he wants to preserve Lewis's centred worlds approach) but to do so he has to give up the first tenet of the Naïve Conception.

A.2. *Decentring: Moss*

According to Moss (2012), whenever the subject believes a relativized proposition or *de se* content (e.g. that her pants are on fire), there is a classical, unrelativized proposition (a *de dicto* content, as she puts it) which the subject also believes, and which is equivalent, in context, to the relativized proposition, given the speaker's background beliefs. Thus suppose that Kaplan thinks: 'My pants are on fire'. He self-ascribes the property $\lambda x.x$'s *pants are on fire*. Since he believes that he is Kaplan (or the author of 'Demonstratives'), he also believes the *de dicto*, uncentred proposition that Kaplan's pants are on fire (or that the pants of the author of 'Demonstratives' are on fire). The two propositions are equivalent *given Kaplan's belief that he is Kaplan (or the author of 'Demonstratives')*, but it is the classical, unrelativized proposition which is communicated to the hearer.

Moss's idea is that the subject's indexical thought is always equivalent in the speaker's mind to some other, non-indexical thought (given what the subject believes). Since it is not indexical, the other thought can be communicated to, and replicated by, those in other contexts. This is an application of Frege's substitution idea, and indeed, Frege's Lauben example from Section 7.2 can be analysed in Moss's framework. Lauben's centred thought that he has been wounded can't be communicated, as Frege points

---

[5] See Weber (2013: S218): 'The problem for the FedEx model arises from centred *utterance* content. The Lewisian account of belief only commits us to centred *belief* content. Perhaps a clash between the two can be avoided by keeping utterance content uncentred.'

out, but given Lauben's belief that he is speaking (i.e. producing the utterance 'I have been wounded'), the initial thought is equivalent to the thought that the speaker has been wounded, and that is the proposition which Lauben's utterance 'I have been wounded' communicates. The whole process we can describe as 'decentring'.

Moss considers as having *de dicto*, uncentred content any thought in which the subject thinks about himself from a third-person perspective. An example she gives is Kaplan looking at himself in the mirror and (not realizing it is himself he is looking at) thinking: 'His pants are on fire'. In this case, she says, the subject thinks about himself in the third-person way and expresses a proposition which is *de dicto* rather than *de se*. Now, Moss points out, the third-person perspective on himself is available to Kaplan even if he realizes that he is the person he sees in the mirror. In this case the subject believes *both* the *de se* proposition and the *de dicto* proposition.

At this point, however, I should register a protest. Kaplan's third-person thought, 'His pants are on fire', is a *demonstrative* thought, a thought about the person Kaplan is looking at in the mirror. Such a thought is as indexical, as centred, as context-bound as the first-person thought 'My pants are on fire'. In Lewis's framework, the subject self-ascribes the property of having his pants on fire in the first case, and the property of looking at a man whose pants are on fire in the second case. There is no significant difference between the two cases, it seems to me.

To overcome the difficulty, Moss has to say that the substitute thoughts are not demonstrative thoughts, but thoughts involving a detached, impersonal way of thinking about the object, e.g. a thought expressible by using a proper name. The thought that Kaplan's pants are on fire fits the bill, it seems. In Moss's framework, however, the contextual equivalence between the substitute thought and the initial thought must be strong enough to preserve subjective probabilities. Moss says that the thoughts should be equivalent 'given what the subject believes *with certainty*'. Since 'Kaplan could always have some shred of doubt about whether he is the man [seen in the mirror] whose pants are on fire, or even about whether he is David Kaplan' (Moss 2012: 229), these identities are not good enough to ground the required equivalence. If the subject is not absolutely certain that he is Kaplan, his thoughts 'My pants are on fire' and 'Kaplan's pants are on fire' will not be equivalent in a sufficiently strong sense. But Moss maintains that for any indexical thought entertained by the speaker, there is a non-indexical thought in the speaker's mind which is equivalent in the strong sense and can substitute for it in communication. Kaplan can always introduce a name for himself, say 'Dr. Demonstrative'. He can *dub* himself. The name is supposed to provide Kaplan with an impersonal way of referring to himself. If Moss is right, 'My pants are on fire' and 'Dr. Demonstrative's pants are on fire' *are* equivalent given what the subject believes with certainty. (The identity 'I am Dr. Demonstrative' is not open to doubt, since it is a stipulation.)

I am not convinced, and I find Moss's argument wanting. Since the name 'Dr. Demonstrative', for Kaplan, is governed by the rule that he uses it to refer to himself, using the name is another way for him to say 'I'. So it is not clear (to me at least) that there are two distinct thoughts here, rather than a single one. But let us assume that Moss is right about 'Dr. Demonstrative' and that the subject accepts both an indexical thought ('My pants are on fire') and an equivalent impersonal thought ('Dr. Demonstrative's pants are on fire'). Following Moss, let us assume that what the subject *communicates* by saying 'My pants are on fire' is the impersonal thought. On the Naïve Conception, the hearer comes to accept the thought the utterance expresses. How does the hearer come to entertain the impersonal thought 'Dr. Demontrative's pants are on fire'? Moss supposes that the speaker tells the hearer: 'let *Dr. Demonstrative* name myself', so as to make her party to the stipulation. But this, Pagin (2016: 289) points out, presupposes that the problem of indexical communication has already been solved. In order to *understand* the stipulation 'let *Dr. Demonstrative* name myself', the hearer must already be capable of understanding first-person utterances by the speaker ('let *Dr. Demonstrative* name myself').

In defence of Moss, I should emphasize that (insofar as I understand her) it does not really matter to her whether the hearer uses the name 'Dr. Demonstrative' in thinking about the speaker, or any other impersonal way of thinking at her disposal. The only thing that matters is that the hearer *gets the reference right*: she must think of the relevant individual, and believe the *de dicto* proposition about him. But what that shows is that

Moss is not really interested in the (fine-grained) *thought* entertained by the hearer, or by the speaker for that matter. (Indeed, she keeps talking about 'propositions', rather than thoughts.) The only thing that matters is that the thought (in context) determines objective truth-conditions, hence a set of possible worlds in which the thought is true. The ordinary possible worlds proposition thus determined may be said to be communicated if the thought entertained by the hearer upon understanding the speaker determines the same truth-conditions in the hearer's context as the speaker's thought in the speaker's context. But to say that is to give up the claim that the speaker's thought has got to be impersonal and uncentred in order for communication to work. The speaker's thought, like the hearer's, may be as indexical and centred as one may wish. The only thing that matters is that the speaker's thought, indexical and centred though it might be, determines in context the same objective truth-conditions as the hearer's thought formed upon understanding the utterance.

I conclude that it is a mistake to think that a thought can have objective truth-conditions only if it is an 'impersonal' thought (assuming such things exist). Indexical thoughts, with their centred contents, do have objective truth-conditions as well, but these truth-conditions are essentially tied to the context in which the thought is tokened (Section 6.1). Instead of attempting to pair each indexical thought with an impersonal thought to account for what is transmitted in communication, it suffices to say that each indexical thought has two levels of content: a relativized proposition or centred content which is the cognitive, internal content of the thought, and a classical, uncentred proposition corresponding to the Austinian proposition and its objective truth-conditions (Recanati 2007). (The Austinian proposition, recall, is nothing but the pair consisting of the centred content and the index of evaluation provided by context; it does the same job as Stalnaker's 'belief state' construed as a pair consisting of a base world and a set of centred worlds.)[6]

---

[6] Weber (2013: S217) acknowledges the theoretical possibility of 'associat[ing] sentences with both centred and uncentred content', and cites two-dimensionalists such as Jackson (1998) and Chalmers (2004) in connection with that view. See also Soames: 'John and Mary express *different beliefs* by sincerely uttering, "I am hungry"—despite the fact that they self-ascribe the *same property*. How does this fit

A.3. Decentring: Stalnaker

Like Moss, Stalnaker (2008) insists that 'ignorance or uncertainty about where one is in the world is always also ignorance or uncertainty about what world one is in' (Stalnaker 2008: 70). In other words, for any centred thought entertained by the thinker, there is an uncentred proposition (an ordinary possible worlds proposition) which captures the truth-conditions of the thought. That uncentred proposition can be used to 'compare the information, including self-locating information, that is available to different subjects',[7] or to the same subject at different times. It can be used to account for disagreement and change of mind, and to account for communication. What is communicated, for Stalnaker, is not the centred content of the subject's thought, but the uncentred content that thought determines, given the identity of the thinker and the time of thought.

I have no quarrel with any of this. As I said, the Austinian proposition (which, again, corresponds to Stalnaker's pair of a base world and a set of centred worlds) determines a classical proposition, which captures the thought's objective truth-conditions. If Stalnaker is right that 'we (as theorists) need to use the same possible worlds to model the various informational states'[8] in play, we can use that classical proposition to do so. We can use it to capture what is objectively communicated, insofar as it is a fundamental constraint on indexical communication that it must preserve truth-conditional content. Using a classical proposition to that effect is compatible with holding that, in communication, the speaker expresses a centred thought, and the hearer comes to accept *another* centred thought (distinct from the speaker's). The constraint will be

---

the idea that *de se* belief is the self-ascription of properties? Pretty well, if we add that an agent x who *self-ascribes* P counts as *ascribing* P of x (but not conversely). Whereas both involve predicating P of x, the former requires *thinking of the predication target in the first-person way* (whatever that amounts to), while that latter doesn't. It will then follow that, in addition to their identical *de se* beliefs, John and Mary also have different *de re* beliefs. [. . .] The same idea allows us to recognize that Lingens and his friend Lola express the same (*de re*) belief when Lingens sincerely says, "This book is about me", and Lola agrees, saying "That book is about you." A state of *de se* believing something is always also a state of *de re* believing something closely related' (Soames 2014: 158–9).

[7] Stalnaker 2008: 65.   [8] Stalnaker 2008: 65.

satisfied, if the speaker's and the hearer's centred thoughts determine the same truth-conditions in their respective contexts. So there is no need to maintain the Naïve Conception to preserve Stalnaker's insight regarding the usefulness of a simultaneous use of centred and uncentred contents in dealing with the dynamics of belief.

One might think that the Naïve Conception is maintained, on Stalnaker's account, since the speaker and the hearer end up believing the same classical proposition as a result of the communicative act. But that is an illusion. As Gibbard says:

It's not [. . .] that the proposition is somehow conveyed from one head to the next. Rather, [. . .] encoding the same proposition is a side effect. It's a side effect of an efficient scheme for transforming and recentering the import of a thought, a scheme that employs thoughts with structure. [. . .] Communication consist[s] in taking a [centred content] and transforming it to center it on the hearer. We accomplish this, however, by forming a thought with a structure, which is then transformed element by element to center on the hearer. For each element of the structured thought, the transformation with recentering preserves reference, and so they preserve the structured proposition signified. (Gibbard 2012: 266–9)

The speaker expresses an indexical thought with centred content. No replication takes place: upon understanding the speaker the hearer comes to entertain another indexical thought, also with centred content. The mechanism at work in communication is what Gibbard describes as 'Transform-and-Recenter'. But the mechanism obeys a constraint of reference preservation, an effect of which is that the speaker's thought and the hearer's thought share their truth-conditions, despite being different thoughts with different centred contents. In this framework,

Th[e] preservation of the proposition . . . is an upshot of communication, and no part of its mechanism. [. . .] 'Communicating' propositions, in the bare sense that the hearer from his standpoint systematically encodes the same proposition as did the speaker from her standpoint, is a by-product of the scheme, not the means by which communication is accomplished. (Gibbard 2012: 268–9)

Communication, in any case, could not simply *be* the transmission of truth-conditional content irrespective of the conceptual vehicles deployed by the conversational protagonists. We saw already in Section 7.1 that for communication to succeed more is needed than the preservation of truth-conditional content: the modes of presentation must be suitably coordinated—the hearer has to think of the reference in the right way.[9]

A.4. *Centred Surrogates: Kölbel and Torre*

Some authors maintain the central assumption of the Naïve Conception, namely, that communicated content must be *shared* by the conversational participants, while, at the same time, taking the shared content in question to be *centred*, rather than uncentred as in Moss's and Stalnaker's frameworks. They exploit Egan's observation that not all centred contents are unshareable: unshareability is the hallmark of centred content only when the speaker and the hearer are in relevantly dissimilar contexts.

Following Weber (2013: S209, fn. 9), let us introduce a bit of terminology. The speaker's first-person thought that his pants are on fire has *malignant* centred content, that is, centred content that is unshareable (in the sense that, if shared, it would determine different truth-conditions in such a way that communication would fail). But in the situation imagined by Egan (Section A.1), the speaker's thought that Sydney is near has *benign* centred content, that is, centred content that is shareable with the hearer, since the hearer's location is close enough to the speaker's. For Kölbel and Torre, the centred content communicated by an utterance such as 'My pants are on fire' is not the (malignant, unshareable) centred content of the subject's thought when he self-ascribes the property that his pants are on fire, but *another*, benign centred content which the speaker and the hearer can share. That content can be represented as another property which (in contrast to the first one) the speaker and the hearer can *both* self-ascribe, e.g. the property of being party to a speech event e such that the speaker of e has burning pants at the time of e. This property, in turn, can be represented either as a set of centred worlds or, as Torre suggests, as a set of *multi-*

---

[9] Gibbard himself makes that point: 'Just thinking the same proposition as the speaker encoded . . . wouldn't by itself be to get what the speaker had said. [. . .] The hearer needs to glean what information is to be had from the sentence spoken and what he knows of its context' (Gibbard 2012: 271). As Gibbard also notes, the same thing holds for remembering (Gibbard 2012: 272).

centred worlds, where both the speaker and the hearer figure in the 'centre'.[10] Whichever option one chooses, we end up with the following claims:

1. The speaker's thought has malignant centred content.
2. The thought communicated to the hearer has benign centred content.

This entails a departure from the Naïve Conception insofar as the speaker's thought is distinct from the communicated thought; but the spirit of the Naïve Conception is retained, for the communicated content, although distinct from the content of the speaker's initial thought, is nevertheless *shared* by the speaker and the hearer. Both the speaker and the hearer self-ascribe (or ascribe to the pair they form) the property of being party to a speech event *e* such that the speaker of *e* has burning pants on fire at the time of *e*.

Kölbel's and Torre's approaches are instances of Frege's *substitution strategy*. What substitutes for the incommunicable content of the speaker's thought is a surrogate content which can be shared. The difference with other instances of the substitution strategy, like that advocated by Moss, is that the surrogate content is centred rather than uncentred: it is a benign centred content.

Kölbel and Torre differ among themselves according to which tenet of the Naïve Conception they reject. What Torre rejects is the first tenet— the 'mind-to-speech' equation:

Speaker's thought = thought expressed by the utterance.

---

[10] Stalnaker (2008) and Ninan (2010) also use multi-centred worlds to account for communication. One reason to go multi-centred, Torre argues, is that 'both conversational participants might know that they both have the property of being party to a speech event *e* such that the speaker of *e* has burning pants at the time of *e* and still not know which of them has the burning pants. That's why we need the additional structure of multicentred worlds' (personal communication). How exactly the multi-centred framework does the trick is a complex issue, which I will not go into here; see Ninan (2010) and Pagin (2016) for discussion. Ninan (2013) emphasizes an advantage of the multi-centred worlds framework when applied to *de re* thoughts (and not merely to communication): it makes it possible to avoid the shortcomings of Lewis's 'centred descriptivism' by extending to thoughts about particular objects what Lewis says of thoughts about oneself.

Torre takes the speaker's thought to have singularly-centred content: the speaker self-ascribes the property an individual has just in case that individual's pants are on fire. But that is not, for Torre, the content *expressed* by the utterance. What the utterance expresses—its potential contribution to the conversational common ground—is a multi-centred content: the property a *sequence of individuals* (comprised of the speaker and the hearer, in that order) has just in case the first member of the sequence (the speaker) has burning pants. As he puts it:

The content of Bond's *assertion* that his pants are on fire is a set of multi-centred worlds, however, the content of Bond's *belief* that he, himself, has flaming pants is a set of singularly-centred worlds. That the belief-transfer model of assertion is not upheld strikes me as a consequence of the fact that different objects are needed to characterize the conversational common ground from those needed to characterize an individual's beliefs (sets of multi-centred worlds versus sets of singularly-centred worlds). (Torre 2010: 112)

In contrast to Torre, Kölbel retains the first tenet of the Naïve Conception: he takes the semantic content of the sentence to be the centred content of the speaker's thought—the set of worlds centred on a person whose pants are on fire. But he rejects the second tenet:

Thought expressed by the utterance = hearer's thought.

For Kölbel, the thought entertained, and accepted, by the understanding hearer is not that (unshareable) centred content but another centred content which is 'locally portable', i.e. shareable (benign). Kölbel calls it the conversational content (CC). What induces the shift from the semantic content to the conversational content is, according to Kölbel, the presence in the sentence of what he calls a 'CC-modifier'. Indexicals such as 'I' are CC-modifiers. A CC-modifier has the effect that, if the centred content expressed by the sentence in which it occurs is not locally portable, what it contributes to the conversation and communicates to the hearer is not that content but a related, locally portable content.

Weber, like Kölbel and unlike Torre, takes the speaker's thought to be semantically expressed, and the communicated thought to result from a recentring operation on it. But he acknowledges that it is possible to 'do things the other way around' (Weber 2013: S210 fn. 11), that is, to give up the first tenet instead of the second one. He discusses the advantages and downsides of the alternative approach, and tentatively concludes that the speaker-centric view (which takes the speaker's thought to be semantically expressed) 'appears to be more natural than the hearer-centric alternative' (Weber 2013: S215). But his discussion is far from conclusive, and one wonders whether the choice is not ultimately arbitrary. This takes us back to the objection I raised to all the views which make that choice: they all accept that one of the points of view involved (that of the speaker or that of the hearer) has got to be privileged, since only one of them can be what the sentence itself expresses. But that claim seems to me dubious and I reject the presupposition of the Naïve Conception. I think there is no such thing as the fine-grained thought expressed by an indexical sentence. I am not denying that such a sentence has a conventional import in virtue of which it makes specific thought contents available in context, but I am denying that one of the thought contents in question has privileged status. In any case, I think the burden of proof is on those who endorse the presupposition.

Torre's multi-centred view fares better than Kölbel's with respect to the arbitrariness criticism, for, like Ninan's very similar view, it has enough resources to avoid privileging speaker over hearer or hearer over speaker. Suppose Kaplan's pants are on fire and he communicates this to Perry. The content of assertion (the multi-centred proposition added to the common ground) is not equivalent to the singularly-centred worlds proposition that one's pants are on fire (the speaker's thought), *but it need not be equated to what the hearer comes to believe either.* What the hearer ultimately comes to believe is a different singularly-centred proposition, that one is being addressed by someone whose pants are on fire. So Torre can evade the arbitrariness charge, by rejecting *both* tenets of the Naïve Conception. He can maintain that the expressed content is neither the speaker's thought nor the hearer's thought. (That is, in effect, what Ninan does.)[11] Still, for Torre, there *is* a proposition which, in communication, is shared by the speaker and the hearer. That proposition is

[11] According to Ninan (2010), the content is one thing for the speaker, and some other thing for the hearer. Ninan keeps the notion of 'the' content of an utterance, however, and construes it as disjunctive.

centred (though not singularly), and it is distinct from the (malignant) centred content of the speaker's thought.

Both Kölbel and Torre see communication as involving a shift, or several shifts, from one centred content to another. They both appeal to a recentring mechanism, similar to that invoked by Gibbard and Weber (whose positions I am about to review). What distinguishes Kölbel and Torre from recentring theorists like Weber and Gibbard is that Kölbel and Torre impose a constraint on the communicated content: it must be shareable. Now, what is that constraint, if not a remnant of the Naïve Conception based on the replication idea? Once we have a recentring process which allows the hearer to adjust the speaker's content to her own needs, what else is needed to account for communication? Here again, the burden of proof is on those who advocate the additional constraint. They have to demonstrate clearly what is gained by having it.

A.5. Recentring and Mental Files: Gibbard

Gibbard (2012) and Weber (2013) abandon the constraint that communicated content must be shareable. They take the speaker's centred thought to be expressed, and the hearer's thought to result from a Transform-and-Recentre operation on it. The only problem I have with their view pertains to the presupposition I have criticized: that one of the thoughts associated with the utterance has to be granted privileged status. Since Gibbard and Weber give up the second tenet of the Naïve Conception (while retaining the presupposition) they give the speaker's thought privileged status. This, I claim, is arbitrary, and I recommend rejecting the presupposition.

In the mental file framework, an indexical (or a referring expression more generally) triggers the search for a referent. It does so in virtue of a conventional feature: the REF feature, which all referential expressions carry (Recanati 1993). The REF feature can be construed as an instruction to the language user: interpreting the expression (or, for the speaker: meaningfully using it) is a matter of mentally referring to some object. Mental reference is done through mental files, so interpreting an expression (or meaningfully using it) requires the language users to associate a mental file with it. Now, in addition to the feature REF, a referential expression carries a descriptive meaning: what I have called the linguistic mode of presentation—certain properties of the reference which are encoded by the expression. 'I' encodes the property of being the speaker, 'you' the property of being the addressee, etc. This sets a constraint on the mental files which the language users are to associate with the expression: the file has to contain the relevant information about the reference of the file—that the referent is producing this utterance, or is the addressee of the person making the utterance, etc. That constraint is a constraint on *all* the files which the conversational participants associate with the expression. Still, the conversational participants are free (and even required) to associate different files with it: the speaker thinks of himself through a SELF file, and the hearer thinks of the speaker through a third-person file (e.g. a demonstrative file). No point of view is privileged. All the relevant files about the speaker (the speaker's first-person file and the hearer's third-person file) contain the information that he is making the utterance, so the constraint is satisfied by all files equally.

What about semantic content? From a strictly linguistic point of view, all the expression carries is the feature REF and the linguistic mode of presentation. In context, when meaningfully used and correctly understood, the expression comes to be associated with two files: the speaker's file and the hearer's file, which *both* satisfy the constraint set by the linguistic mode of presentation. The expression then acquires a sense for *each* of the two subjects (namely the mental file each of them associates with it), and it acquires a reference, namely the reference of the associated files.

Referential communication succeeds only if the files converge on the same object. In context, other constraints than that carried by the linguistic mode of presentation will have to be satisfied by the interpreter's files to match the speaker's file and corefer with it.[12] In Loar's example, satisfaction of the (meagre) linguistic mode of presentation carried by the pronoun 'he'

---

[12] See Section 7.2, note 12. Because there are other constraints than those carried by the linguistic mode of presentation, I am not particularly worried by the alleged counterexample to my theory put forward by Sajed Tayebi in 'Recanati on Communication of First-Person Thoughts' (Tayebi 2012).

(to the effect that the referent is male) is not sufficient: the hearer has to think of the referent as the man on television, since that is what the speaker has in mind. This constraint of match is nothing but a consequence of the more general constraint on referential communication, that mental files must corefer. The hearer must understand who the speaker is referring to, in order to mentally refer to the same object. The linguistic mode of presentation provides a clue, but the hearer has to rely on contextual factors in most cases (Burge 2003b: 380, Buchanan 2014: §5). The contextual factors in question play a role in further constraining the files in the hearer's mind.[13]

Gibbard has a role for mental files in his framework. The 'transform' part of the global Transform-and-Recentre operation operates on *concepts*, which are constituents of structured thoughts. Gibbard describes communication as follows:

A sentence encodes a thought which, in the first place, is centred: a true thought gives some aspect of how the world is from the thinker's standpoint. It gives a property of her standpoint. The hearer thus learns something of how things are from the speaker's standpoint, and he, knowing much or little about the speaker's standpoint, transforms the thought to center it on himself, thus updating his view of how things are from his own standpoint. *The way he does this, however, depends on the thought's being structured. He transforms each of the conceptual elements of the thought in a way that preserves reference.* For each transformed concept, that is to say, its reference from the hearer's standpoint is the same as the reference of the original concept from the speaker's standpoint.   (Gibbard 2012: 271, emphasis mine)

What are these concepts which get transformed in the recentring process? They sound very much like mental files. Gibbard talks of 'individual concepts' and gives as examples individual concepts like 'the first-person

[13] If the hearer disregards the contextual clues (as in Heck's version of the Perry example, cited in Section 7.1, note 6), or misinterprets them (as in Loar's example, discussed in that same section), the chances of coreferring are significantly diminished. The phenomenon of *deviant coreference* illustrated by these and other philosophical examples corresponds to cases in which the hearer corefers with the speaker by sheer luck. That is not *justified coreference*, and is not sufficient to ground successful communication (Gibbard 2012: 267). (On the role of epistemological considerations in the theory of referential communication, see Heck 1995 and Dickie 2015.)

concept i' and 'the present time concept t'. When Ann sincerely writes in her letter, 'I am happy', the thought she voices consists of these two concepts joined by the 'be happy at' two-place relational concept H. So Ann thinks (and expresses) the structured thought *Hit* (Gibbard 2012: 257–9). If Ben, who reads the letter, does not know who wrote it, he

forms a concept of the letter-writer, [which he] might voice to himself as 'that woman'. It is an individual concept which from his standpoint picks out the writer and denotes her rigidly. He likewise forms a concept of the time of writing, which from his standpoint rigidly picks out the time of writing. When he says to himself, 'that woman was happy then', his phrase 'that woman' voices the concept of whatever woman wrote the letter one is reading. [...] What writer Ann voices with 'I' reader Ben thus transforms into a concept he voices with 'that woman', and he recenters this transformed concept on himself. Likewise with time: Ben's word 'then' voices, in this utterance, the concept of whenever this letter was written, again taken rigidly. What Ann voiced with 'now' and the present tense Ben transforms into what he voices with 'then', and he centers this on himself now.   (Gibbard 2012: 266–7)

Gibbard says that Ben (the hearer) transforms the first-person concept expressed by the speaker into his third-person THAT WOMAN concept, and recentres the latter concept on himself. But what does it mean to talk of recentring a *concept* (a vehicle)? In the mental file framework, that makes sense. Since files are based on ER relations to the owner of the file, deployment of the file means that the subject bears such and such a relation to the reference. The files carry presuppositional content, which corresponds to the diagonal of the concept's character in Gibbard's framework.[14] In the case of the first-person concept, the ER relation is identity; in the case of Ben's individual concept 'that woman', the ER relation is that of reading a letter she wrote. On the presuppositional mode, the speaker self-ascribes the former relation (identity) to the referent, while the hearer self-ascribes the other relation (that of reading a letter the referent

[14] Concepts and structured thoughts, for Gibbard as for Perry, have characters. Characters, Gibbard says, are functions from standpoint and world thought about to reference, and the unstructured import of a thought is the diagonal of the character, construed as a centred content. We can also talk of the import of a concept. The import of a concept is a centred content, corresponding to the diagonal of the concept's character.

wrote). These presuppositional self-ascriptions have centred content, just as the at-issue self-ascription of happiness. But the centre (the person to whom the presupposed centred content is self-ascribed) shifts: the first-person concept in the speaker's thought is centred on the speaker, while the third-person concept in the hearer's thought is centred on the hearer.[15]

The presuppositional content carried by a deployment of the file is its contribution to the internal content of the thought (Section 6.2). The internal content accounts for behaviour, as we saw, while the reference of the file, and the truth-conditions of the thought, depend upon the external factor (which object, if any, stands at the other end of the putative ER relation). This dual structure is apparent in Gibbard's account:

A twin-Ben on twin-Earth reading a twin letter from twin-Ann would have the same structured thoughts as does Ben. Twin-Ben's phrase 'that woman' (or his world 'she'), however, on this occasion, denotes not Ann but twin-Ann. As with Ben, moreover, twin-Ben's phrase 'that woman' is rigid, denoting the same person, twin-Ann, when applied to counterfactual scenarios.   (Gibbard 2012: 268)

The rigidity of Gibbard's individual concepts is also accounted for on the assumption that these concepts are files. Files refer through the ER relations they are based on. These relations hold in the actual world,

---

[15] The object to which the property 'Happy' is ascribed is the relatum of the ER relation—the reference of the file. In the first-person case the relatum is the subject, so the at-issue ascription is a *self*-ascription (of happiness). But in the third-person case, when the hearer Ben interprets the utterance 'I am happy', the relatum of the relevant ER relation is not the subject, Ben himself, but the person who wrote the letter (Mary). The ascription of happiness is to that person. There is no *at-issue self-ascription* in this case, but only a *presuppositional self-ascription* (of the property of bearing the relevant relation [reading a letter she wrote] to some person y, who happens to be Mary). Another way of looking at the situation: the at-issue ascription is *de re* in all cases, and its target (the relevant *res*) is the relatum of the presupposed ER relation. The *de re* ascription counts as a *self*-ascription when, and only when, the presupposed ER relation is identity. But the underlying, presuppositional self-ascription, through which the referent y is introduced, *is* a self-ascription in all cases. Since the target of the at-issue ascription is the object y introduced through the presuppositional self-ascription, we retain the essentials of the Lewis–Chisholm picture: every *de re* thought is *de se*, at the most basic level. Separating the presuppositional self-ascription and the at-issue *de re* ascription (which may or may not also be a self-ascription) makes it possible to construe the latter as anaphoric on the former. (On the relations between anaphora and the *de se*, see Higginbotham 2009.)

and they are not affected by counterfactual suppositions. Counterfactual suppositions are about the reference of the file, and the reference of the file is fixed by its actual-world relations to entities in the environment, not by the relations that would hold were the counterfactual scenario true.

I conclude that Gibbard's story can easily be reformulated in the mental file framework. If we do so, the alleged primacy of the speaker's point of view reduces to the trivial fact that the speaker's thought comes first: the speaker first voices her structured thought (involving the deployment of her SELF file), and then, in interpreting the utterance, the hearer deploys his own, third-person file in understanding the speaker. I don't think we need to read more into Gibbard's claim that the hearer 'transforms' the concept voiced by the speaker. In particular, the speaker's concept (her SELF file), or the structured thought of which it is a constituent, need not be seen as the input to the mental process through which the hearer comes to entertain his own thought. The input to the hearer's interpretive process is the utterance. The fact that the utterance contains a referring expression leads the hearer to activate a file, constrained by the linguistic mode of presentation encoded by the expression. The hearer does not literally 'transform' the individual concept (the file) deployed by the speaker. He simply comes up with a different concept (a different file) as a result of interpreting the utterance. The starting point of the interpretation process is not the speaker's thought allegedly expressed by the utterance, but linguistic properties of the utterance such as the REF feature and the linguistic mode of presentation (together with contextual facts such as the direction of the speaker's gaze, what the conversation is about, etc.).

A.6. Weber's Recentring Model

Weber's theory of recentring is very similar to Gibbard's. According to Weber:

The speaker literally expresses one of her beliefs. The belief the hearer acquires, however, is not the one expressed by the utterance. Rather, she acquires a content that is related in a certain way to the utterance content. The acquired content is determined by the content expressed by the speaker together with the hearer's beliefs about how she is related to the speaker's context.   (Weber 2013: S206)

The Recentring Model he puts forwards (Weber 2013: S212) involves four main steps:

The Recentring Model

1. The hearer perceives an utterance 'u'. [*Perceiving.*]
2. The hearer believes that the expressed content of 'u' is true of the speaker. [*Centring.*]
3. The hearer believes that she is R-related to the speaker. [*Locating.*]
4. The hearer infers information about herself from 2. and 3. [*Recentring.*]

The Centring step itself is decomposed into two separate steps, which Weber calls *Understanding* and *Trusting*:

Firstly, to gain information from an utterance, the hearer has to understand it. For us this means that she has to know what the expressed content of 'u' is. Secondly, in the standard case of communication, the hearer will trust the speaker, i.e. she will believe that the speaker has made a true utterance. [...] To trust the speaker is to believe that the utterance correctly characterizes the speaker's context. Putting the *Understanding* and the *Trusting* step together, we get the *Centering* step: the hearer believes that the expressed content of "u" is true of the speaker's context.   (Weber 2013: S212)

Pagin (2016) objects to Weber's model that it presupposes something false: that the hearer, in order to understand the utterance, has to believe the speaker. The Centring step requires two things of the hearer, according to Weber: (i) she must grasp the centred content expressed by the utterance (*Understanding*), and (ii) she must believe that that content adequately characterizes the speaker, that is, is true of him (*Trusting*). Pagin objects that *Trusting*

cannot be in general required, or we could not make sense of exchanges like the following:

(36)   A: You have Groat's disease.

       B: I don't believe that./That's not true.

In communication we typically first understand what the content of a speaker's utterance is, and then assess it as true or false with respect to the actual evaluation point. [. . .] However, on a centred contents model, there is no centred content that both concerns the subject from a *de se* perspective and is only entertained, not believed. This is so, since on Lewis's model, it is only insofar as a centred content is self-ascribed by a subject that a property is predicated of the subject at all. The predication of the property is not part of the content; it enters only in the self-ascription step, which is the centred content counterpart to ordinary belief. Without going non-centred, and adding a representation of the subject in the content itself, the subject cannot grasp without belief what is predicated of her. This short-coming does not matter as long as we are only concerned with belief itself, as Lewis was, but in communication we come across contents that we may believe or not.   (Pagin 2016: 299)

How is this problem to be solved? Weber's model has clearly to be revised to maintain the required gap between understanding and believing. What the hearer has to do is not to trust the hearer but to reach a level of *pragmatic understanding* of the speaker's utterance: she has to understand that the speaker is self-ascribing a certain property, without taking a stance on whether or not the self-ascription is true.[16]

To understand that the speaker is self-ascribing a property, the hearer has to think about the speaker. Pragmatic understanding involves, on the hearer's part, a representation of the speaker. In the centred worlds framework that is a self-ascription, by the hearer, of a relation R to the speaker. That is Weber's *Locating* step. So the second revision I recommend to his model consists in taking the *Locating* step prior to achieving the second step of *Centring* (*Pragmatic Understanding*, which now substitutes for *Trusting*).[17] When we put together the two revisions, we get the following model:

---

[16] What I call 'Pragmatic Understanding' is what Pagin calls 'Extended Understanding'.

[17] Gibbard insists that the *Locating* step occurs at a very early stage. See Gibbard 2012: 259.

The Revised Recentring Model

1. The hearer perceives an utterance 'u'. [*Perceiving.*]
2. The hearer grasps the centred content expressed by 'u': a certain property Φ. [*Linguistic understanding.*]
3. The hearer believes that she is R-related to the speaker of 'u'. [*Locating.*]
4. The hearer understands that the speaker (the person she is R-related to) is self-ascribing the expressed content of 'u', namely the property Φ. [*Pragmatic understanding.*]
5. The hearer concludes that if 'u' is true, she is R-related to someone who has the property Φ. [*Conditional Recentring.*]

Communication has now been achieved, and the hearer can decide whether or not she wants to trust the speaker and believe the communicated information, namely, that she is R-related to someone who has property Φ. If she trusts the speaker, she will self-ascribe that property (the property of being R-related to some Φ) by detaching the consequent of the conditional in *Conditional Recentring*. In the revised model, the distinction between the understanding stage and the believing stage emphasized by Pagin has been respected even though the contents involved throughout are centred contents.

Pagin thinks there still is a problem, however. In the dialogue about Groat's disease, B's response ('I don't believe that'/'That's not true') indicates that B has grasped the content communicated by A, yet refuses to endorse it. But how, in the centred worlds framework, can B grasp the content that he has Groat disease, without actually endorsing it? Note that, in line with the framework, step 5 (Conditional Recentring) ought to be couched as a self-ascription of properties. Pagin proposes that the property self-ascribed by B at step 5 is the conditional property of *having Groat's disease if u is true*. Pagin now objects:

In order to isolate the content that *he, B, has Groat's disease*, B must detach by modus ponens, but this again means *accepting* the premise that the [utterance] is [true]...It is an inherent limitation of the centred content framework that (unembedded) contents cannot be self-predicated without being self-ascribed, i.e. believed. Thus, only in the world of the hyper-gullible, who accept a content even before knowing what it is, can centred contents with Weber's recentering offer a model of communication. (Pagin 2016: 301)

Pagin is right that, in the centred worlds framework, there is no way in which B can grasp-without-believing the *de se* content intuitively communicated to him, namely that he, B, has Groat's disease. That is so because, 'on a centred contents model, there is no centred content that both concerns the subject from a *de se* perspective *and* is only entertained, not believed' (Pagin 2016: 27). Yet the difficulty should not be exaggerated. The centred content theorist can simply bite the bullet: what substitutes for B's grasping-without-believing the *de se* proposition that he has Groat's disease is B's self-ascribing the conditional property (having Groat's disease if u is true). *As soon as B self-ascribes the conditional property, he has understood the utterance.* To go beyond that and actually self-ascribe the property of having Groat's disease, B needs to trust A and take her utterance to be true.

Does that mean that B is hyper-gullible and accepts a content even before knowing what it is? I do not think so. The centred content theorist rejects the standard content/force distinction, but there is something that acts as proxy for it: the distinction between understanding (self-ascribing the conditional property) and accepting (self-ascribing the detached property). Accepting *is* trusting, but understanding does not presuppose trusting. To be sure, a consequence of the theory is that the content which the hearer accepts (the detached property) is not the same thing as what he grasps (the conditional property). But an independent argument is needed to show that that consequence (and therefore the theory) is unacceptable. Pagin does not provide such an argument, and his case seems to rest on the standard content/force distinction, which his opponent rejects. So I see no reason to deny the centred content theorist the right to embrace the following view: what the hearer grasps (the conditional property he self-ascribes) is an intermediate level of content between the thought expressed by the speaker (the property she self-ascribes) and the thought the trusting hearer arrives at (the detached property he self-ascribes).

A.7. *The Metarepresentational Stance*

Pagin raises another issue in discussing Weber's model:

Weber suggests [. . .] that interpretation by the hearer is metalinguistic and meta-doxastic; the hearer does not get the content from the speaker . . . A number of meta-doxastic inference steps must be performed in order in order to arrive at the self-ascriptions that are the basis for the responses in (36B). [...] [It is] very implausible that interpretation ever works like this.   (Pagin 2016: 302)

It is true that the *Pragmatic Understanding* step is metarepresentational; the hearer ascribes an attitude to the speaker, towards the content expressed by the utterance. I mentioned Dummett's solution to the problem of indexical communication (Section 7.2). For him, communication is not the replication of thought, but the *recognition* of (the speaker's) thought. The *Pragmatic Understanding* step involves recognition of the speaker's thought at the attitudinal level and not merely at the level of content.

Metarepresentational approaches to communication are far from uncommon. One of the leading theories of communication, Grice's, is couched in explicitly metarepresentational terms. Among the followers of Grice, some have insisted that human communication is essentially metarepresentational (Sperber 1994, 2000, Sperber and Wilson 2002). But there is another approach (or family of approaches) to communication, which stresses its direct, non-inferential character and likens it to perception. Reid (1970), McDowell (1980, 1993), Burge (1993), and Millikan (1984), to name only a few, have eloquently argued for such views. I myself have argued for the direct, non-inferential approach (Recanati 2002), so I understand Pagin's worry that Weber's model forces the inferential/metarepresentational approach on us.

The mental file approach does not require metarepresentations: in principle, the hearer goes directly from the utterance and the context to the thought she entertains when she understands the utterance. The metarepresentation of the speaker's attitude is not a prerequisite for understanding, in a framework which gives up the primacy of the speaker's point of view. At the same time, it would make no sense to deny the important role of metarepresentations in communication, which the Gricean tradition rightly emphasizes. In Section A.5, I mentioned the role of contextual clues in achieving coreference with the speaker. The contextual information which needs to be tapped is, to a very large extent, metarepresentational: it is information about what the speaker is up to. So we do need metarepresentations, *in addition to* 'direct' understanding.

The mental file framework provides the metarepresentations, without making them a prerequisite for understanding, so it strikes the right balance between the two families of approaches. The metarepresentations are provided through the mechanism of 'indexed files' (briefly described in Section 3.2). An indexed file is a file that stands, in the subject's mind, for some other subject's file about the referent. An indexed file is linked in the subject's mind to the regular file she has about the referent, and an indexed file only refers through its link to a regular file in the speaker's mind. There is also the possibility for an indexed file to be 'free-wheeling', that is, unlinked to any regular file in the speaker's mind. Such files do not refer but they are useful in representing the doxastic alternatives of a subject whose ontology we do not share.[18]

Indexed files are used in metarepresenting the attitudes of other agents, and specifically in representing the way they think about the objects their attitudes are about. They provide a flexible and powerful framework for dealing with opacity issues. But they are relevant also to the present topic. The *Pragmatic Understanding* step involves a metarepresentation: a representation of the subject's self-ascription of the property Φ. In the mental file framework, the metarepresentation in the hearer's mind takes the form of a SELF file indexed to the speaker. When the speaker says 'I am happy', the hearer not only feeds the information 'Happy' into his third-person file about the speaker (based on the R relation Weber talks about), but he also feeds that same information into the indexed file which, in the hearer's mind, stands for the speaker's SELF file. There is, at the same time, direct information transfer (the information 'Happy' goes into the third-person file associated for the hearer with the word 'I' uttered by the speaker, without any mediation) *and* metarepresentation (the hearer represents the speaker's self-ascription, by feeding the information into the SELF file indexed to the speaker).

[18] On indexed files and their role in the development of metarepresentational capacities, see Perner et al. 2015.

References

Bach, K. (1987) *Thought and Reference*. Oxford: Clarendon Press.

Ball, D. (2015) Indexicality, Transparency, and Mental Files. *Inquiry* 58: 353–67.

Barwise, J. (1989) Situations, Facts, and True Propositions. In his *The Situation in Logic*, 221–54. Stanford: CSLI Publications.

Barwise, J. and Etchemendy, J. (1987) *The Liar: An Essay on Truth and Circularity*. New York: Oxford University Press.

Berger, A. (2002) *Terms and Truth: Reference Direct and Anaphoric*. Cambridge, MA: MIT Press.

Bezuidenhout, A. (1997) The Communication of De Re Thoughts. *Noûs* 31: 197–225.

Branquinho, J. (1999) The Problem of Cognitive Dynamics. *Grazer Philosophische Studien* 56: 2–15.

Branquinho, J. (2008) On the Persistence of Indexical Belief. *Proceedings of the XXII World Congress of Philosophy* 39: 21–30.

Buchanan, R. (2014) Reference, Understanding and Communication. *Australasian Journal of Philosophy* 92: 55–70.

Burge, T. (1974) Demonstrative Constructions, Reference, and Truth. *Journal of Philosophy* 71: 205–23.

Burge, T. (1979) Sinning Against Frege. *Philosophical Review* 88: 398–432.

Burge, T. (1983) Russell's Problem and Intentional Identity. In J. Tomberlin (ed.) *Agent, Language, and the Structure of the World*, 79–110. Indianapolis: Hackett Publishing Company.

Burge, T. (1993) Content Preservation. *Philosophical Review* 102: 547–88.

Burge, T. (2003a) Memory and Persons. *Philosophical Review* 112: 289–337.

Burge, T. (2003b) Tracking Perspectives: Reply to Higginbotham. In M. Hahn and B. Ramberg (eds) *Reflections and Replies: Essays on the Philosophy of Tyler Burge*, 377–82. Cambridge, MA: MIT Press/Bradford Books.

Büring, D. (2005) *Binding Theory*. Cambridge: Cambridge University Press.

Campbell, J. (1987) Is Sense Transparent? *Proceedings of the Aristotelian Society* 88: 273–92.

Campbell, J. (1994) *Past, Space and Self.* Cambridge, MA: MIT Press.

Castañeda, H.-N. (1999) *The Phenomeno-Logic of the I: Essays on Self-Consciousness,* ed. J. Hart and T. Kapitan. Bloomington: Indiana University Press.

Chalmers, D. (2004) Epistemic Two-Dimensional Semantics. *Philosophical Studies* 118: 153–226.

Chastain, C. (1975) Reference and Context. In K. Gunderson (ed.) *Language, Mind, and Knowledge,* 194–269. Minneapolis: University of Minnesota Press.

Crimmins, M. and Perry, J. (1989) The Prince and the Phone Booth. *Journal of Philosophy* 86: 685–711.

Cumming, S. (2013) From Coordination to Content. *Philosopher's Imprint* 13(4): 1–16.

Davies, M. (1982) Individuation and the Semantics of Demonstratives. *Journal of Philosophical Logic* 11: 287–310.

Devitt, M. (1981) *Designation.* New York: Columbia University Press.

Devitt, M. (2015) Should Proper Names Still Seem So Problematic? In A. Bianchi (ed.) *On Reference,* 108–43. Oxford: Oxford University Press.

Dickie, I. (2015) *Fixing Reference.* Oxford: Oxford University Press.

Dickie, I. and Rattan, G. (2010) Sense, Communication, and Rational Engagement. *Dialectica* 64: 131–51.

Dokic, J. (1996) The Dynamics of Deictic Thoughts. *Philosophical Studies* 82: 179–204.

Donnellan, K. (1966) Reference and Definite Descriptions. *Philosophical Review* 75: 281–304. Reprinted in S. Schwartz (ed.) *Naming, Necessity and Natural Kinds,* 42–65. Ithaca: Cornell University Press, 1977.

Drapeau Vieira Contim, F. (2016) Mental Files and Non-Transitive *De Jure* Coreference. *Review of Philosophy and Psychology* 7: 365–88.

Dummett, M. (1978) *Truth and Other Enigmas.* London: Duckworth.

Dummett, M. (1981) *The Interpretation of Frege's Philosophy.* London: Duckworth.

Dummett, M. (1993) *The Seas of Language.* Oxford: Clarendon Press.

Egan, A. (2007) Epistemic Modals, Relativism and Assertion. *Philosophical Studies* 133: 1–22.

Evans, G. (1973) The Causal Theory of Names. *Proceedings of the Aristotelian Society,* Supp. Vol. 47: 187–208. Reprinted in Evans (1985), 1–24.

Evans, G. (1980) Pronouns. *Linguistic Inquiry* 11: 337–62. Reprinted in Evans (1985), 214–48.

Evans, G. (1981) Understanding Demonstratives. In H. Parret and J. Bouveresse (eds) *Meaning and Understanding*, 280–303. Berlin: De Gruyter. Reprinted in Evans (1985), 291–321.

Evans, G. (1982) *The Varieties of Reference*, ed. J. McDowell. Oxford: Clarendon Press.

Evans, G. (1985) *Collected Papers*. Oxford: Clarendon Press.

Fauconnier, G. (1974) *La Coréférence: Syntaxe ou Sémantique?* Paris: Seuil.

Field, H. (1973) Theory Change and the Indeterminacy of Reference. *Journal of Philosophy* 70: 462–81.

Fiengo, R. and May, R. (1994) *Indices and Identity*. Cambridge, MA: MIT Press/Bradford Books.

Fiengo, R. and May, R. (1996) Anaphora and Identity. In S. Lappin (ed.) *Handbook of Contemporary Semantic Theory*, 117–44. Oxford: Blackwell.

Fiengo, R. and May, R. (1998) Names and Expressions. *Journal of Philosophy* 95: 377–409.

Fiengo, R. and May, R. (2006) De Lingua *Belief*. Cambridge, MA: MIT Press/Bradford Books.

Fine, K. (2007) *Semantic Relationism*. Oxford: Blackwell.

Fine, K. (2010) Reply to Lawlor's 'Varieties of Coreference'. *Philosophy and Phenomenological Research* 81: 496–501.

Fodor, J. (1995) *The Elm and the Expert*. Cambridge, MA: MIT Press/Bradford Books.

Fodor, J. (2003) *Hume Variations*. Oxford: Clarendon Press.

Fodor, J. and Pylyshyn, Z. (1988) Connectionism and Cognitive Architecture: A Critical Analysis. *Cognition* 28: 3–71.

Frege, G. (1967a) *Kleine Schriften*, ed. I. Angelelli. Hildesheim: Olms.

Frege, G. (1967b) The Thought: A Logical Enquiry, English trans. by A. and M. Quinton. In P. Strawson (ed.) *Philosophical Logic*, 17–38. Oxford: Oxford University Press.

Garcia-Carpintero, M. (2000) A Presuppositional Account of Reference-Fixing. *Journal of Philosophy* 97: 109–47.

Garcia-Carpintero, M. (2006) Two-Dimensionalism: A Neo-Fregean Interpretation. In M. Garcia-Carpintero and J. Macia (eds) *Two-Dimensional Semantics*, 181–204. Oxford: Clarendon Press.

Garcia-Carpintero, M. (2016) Token-Reflexive Presuppositions and the *De Se*. In M. Garcia-Carpintero and S. Torre (eds) *About Oneself*, 179–99. Oxford: Oxford University Press.

Geach, P. (1955) Review of Mates 1953. *Philosophical Review* 64: 143–5.

Geach, P. (1967) Intentional Identity. *Journal of Philosophy* 74: 627–32.

Geach, P. (1969) The Perils of Pauline. Reprinted in P. Geach (1972) *Logic Matters*, 153–65. Oxford: Blackwell.

Gibbard, A. (2012) *Meaning and Normativity*. Oxford: Oxford University Press.

Goodsell, T. (2014) Is *De Jure* Coreference Non-Transitive? *Philosophical Studies* 167: 291–312.

Gray, A. (2016) Minimal Descriptivism. *Review of Philosophy and Psychology* 7: 343–64.

Grice, P. (1969) Vacuous Names. In D. Davidson and J. Hintikka (eds) *Words and Objections*, 118–45. Dordrecht: Reidel.

Hawley, K. (2001) *How Things Persist*. Oxford: Oxford University Press.

Heck, R. (1995) The Sense of Communication. *Mind* 104: 79–106.

Heck, R. (2002) Do Demonstratives Have Senses? *Philosopher's Imprint* 2: 1–33.

Heck, R. (2012) Solving Frege's Puzzle. *Journal of Philosophy* 109: 132–74.

Hedden, B. (2015a) Time-Slice Rationality. *Mind* 124: 449–91.

Hedden, B. (2015b) *Reasons without Persons: Rationality, Identity, and Time*. Oxford: Oxford University Press.

Heim, I. (1998) Anaphora and Semantic Interpretation: A Reinterpretation of Reinhart's Approach. In U. Sauerland and O. Percus (eds) *The Interpretive Tract* (MIT Working Papers in Linguistics, 25), 205–46.

Higginbotham, J. (1985) On Semantics. *Linguistic Inquiry* 16: 547–93.

Higginbotham, J. (2003) Competence with Demonstratives. In M. Hahn and B. Ramberg (eds) *Reflections and Replies: Essays on the Philosophy of Tyler Burge*, 101–15. Cambridge, MA: MIT Press/Bradford Books.

Higginbotham, J. (2009) *Tense, Aspect, and Indexicality*. Oxford: Oxford University Press.

Hintikka, J. (1973) *Time and Necessity: Studies in Aristotle's Theory of Modality*. Oxford: Clarendon Press.

Jackson, F. (1998) *From Metaphysics to Ethics*. Oxford: Clarendon Press.

Kamp, H. (1990) Prolegomena to a Structural Theory of Belief and Other Attitudes. In C.A. Anderson and J. Owens (eds) *Propositional Attitudes*, 27–90. Stanford: CSLI.

Kamp, H. (2015) Using Proper Names as Intermediaries between Labelled Entity Representations. *Erkenntnis* 80: 263–312.

Kamp, H. and Reyle, U. (1993) *From Discourse to Logic*. Dordrecht: Kluwer.

Kaplan, D. (1989a) Demonstratives. In J. Almog, H. Wettstein, and J. Perry (eds), *Themes from Kaplan*, 481–563. New York: Oxford University Press.

Kaplan, D. (1989b) Afterthoughts. In J. Almog, H. Wettstein, and J. Perry (eds), *Themes from Kaplan*, 565–614. New York: Oxford University Press.

Karttunen, L. (1976) Discourse Referents. *Syntax and Semantics* 7: 363–85.

Kehler, A. (2002) *Coherence, Reference, and the Theory of Grammar*. Stanford: CSLI.

Kneale, W. and Kneale, M. (1962) *The Development of Logic*. Oxford: Clarendon Press.

Kölbel, M. (2013) The Conversational Role of Centred Content. *Inquiry* 56: 97–121.

Kripke, S. (1977) Speaker's Reference and Semantic Reference. *Midwest Studies in Philosophy* 2: 255–76.

Kripke, S. (1980) *Naming and Necessity*. Oxford: Blackwell.

Lasersohn, P. (1999) Pragmatic Halos. *Language* 75: 522–51.

Lasnik, H. (1976) Remarks on Coreference. *Linguistic Analysis* 2: 1–22.

Lawlor, K. (2001) *New Thoughts about Old Things*. New York: Garland.

Lawlor, K. (2010) Varieties of Coreference. *Philosophy and Phenomenological Research* 81: 485–501.

Lewis, D. (1976) Survival and Identity. In A. Rorty (ed.) *The Identities of Persons*, 17–40. Berkeley: University of California Press.

Lewis, D. (1979) Attitudes *De Dicto* and *De Se*. *Philosophical Review* 88: 513–43. Reprinted (with a postscript) in Lewis (1983) *Philosophical Papers*, vol. 1, 133–59, New York: Oxford University Press.

Loar, B. (1976) The Semantics of Singular Terms. *Philosophical Studies* 30: 353–77.

Lockwood, M. (1971) Identity and Reference. In M. Munitz (ed.) *Identity and Individuation*, 199–211. New York: New York University Press.

Mates, B. (1953) *Stoic Logic*. Berkeley: University of California Press.

Matthen, M. (2010) Is Memory Preservation? *Philosophical Studies* 148: 3–14.

McDowell, J. (1980) Meaning, Communication, and Knowledge. In Z. van Straaten (ed.) *Philosophical Subjects: Essays Presented to P.F. Strawson*, 117–39. Oxford: Clarendon Press.

McDowell, J. (1993) Knowledge by Hearsay. In B. Matilal and A. Chakrabarti (eds) *Knowing From Words: Western and Indian Philosophical Analysis of Understanding and Testimony*, 195–224. Dordrecht: Kluwer.

McGinn, C. (1982) The Structure of Content. In A. Woodfield (ed.) *Thought and Object*, 207–58. Oxford: Clarendon Press.

Millikan, R. (1984) *Language, Thought, and Other Biological Categories*. Cambridge, MA: MIT Press.

Millikan, R. (1997) Images of Identity: In Search of Modes of Presentation. *Mind* 106: 499–519.

Millikan, R. (2000) *On Clear and Confused Ideas*. Cambridge: Cambridge University Press.

Moss, S. (2012) Updating as Communication. *Philosophy and Phenomenological Research* 85: 225–48.

Moss, S. (2015) Time-Slice Epistemology and Action Under Indeterminacy. *Oxford Studies in Epistemology* 5: 172–94.

Neale, S. (2005) Pragmatism and Binding. In Z. Szabo (ed.) *Semantics versus Pragmatics*, 165–285. Oxford: Clarendon Press.

Ninan, D. (2008) *Imagination, Content, and the Self*. PhD dissertation, MIT.

Ninan, D. (2010) *De Se* Attitudes: Ascription and Communication. *Philosophy Compass* 5: 551–67.

Ninan, D. (2013) Self-Location and Other-Location. *Philosophy and Phenomenological Research* 87: 330–1.

Ninan, D. (2015) On Recanati's *Mental Files*. *Inquiry* 58: 368–77.

Onofri, D. (2015) Mental Files and Rational Inferences. *Inquiry* 58: 378–92.

Pagin, P. (2016) *De Se* Communication: Centred or Uncentred? In M. Garcia-Carpintero and S. Torre (eds) *About Oneself*, 272–306. Oxford: Oxford University Press.

Papineau, D. (2006) Phenomenal and Perceptual Concepts. In Alter, T. and Walter, S. (eds) *Phenomenal Concepts and Phenomenal Knowledge: New Essays on Consciousness and Physicalism*, 111–44. New York: Oxford University Press.

Papineau, D. (2013) Comments on François Recanati's *Mental Files*: Doubts about Indexicality. In F. Salis (ed.) *Book Symposium on François Recanati's Mental Files*, 159–76. *Disputatio* 5/36.

Patel-Grosz, P. (2012) *(Anti-)Locality at the Interfaces*. PhD dissertation, MIT.

Perner, J., Huemer, M., and Leahy, B. (2015) Mental Files and Belief: A Cognitive Theory of How Children Represent Belief and Its Intentionality. *Cognition* 145: 77–88.

Perry, J. (1977) Frege on Demonstratives. *Philosophical Review* 86: 474–97, reprinted, with a postscript, in Perry (1993), 3–32.

Perry, J. (1979) The Problem of the Essential Indexical. *Noûs* 13: 3–21, reprinted, with a postscript, in Perry (1993), 33–52.

Perry, J. (1980a) A Problem about Continued Belief. *Pacific Philosophical Quarterly* 61: 317–32, reprinted, with a postscript, in Perry (1993), 69–90.

Perry, J. (1980b) Belief and Acceptance. *Midwest Studies in Philosophy* 5: 533–42, reprinted, with a postscript, in Perry (1993), 53–67.

Perry, J. (1988) Cognitive Significance and New Theories of Reference. *Noûs* 22: 1–18.

Perry, J. (1993) *The Problem of the Essential Indexical and Other Essays*. New York: Oxford University Press.

Perry, J. (1997) Rip Van Winkle and Other Characters. *European Review of Philosophy* 2: 13–39. Reprinted in Perry (2000), 355–76.

Perry, J. (2000) *The Problem of the Essential Indexical and Other Essays*, expanded edition. Stanford: CSLI.

Perry, J. (2001) *Knowledge, Possibility and Consciousness*. Cambridge, MA: MIT Press/Bradford Books.

Perry, J. (2006) Stalnaker and Indexical Belief. In J. Thomson and A. Byrne (eds) *Content and Modality: Themes from the Philosophy of Robert Stalnaker*, 204–21. Oxford: Clarendon Press.

Perry, J. (2012a) Thinking about the Self. In J. Liu and J. Perry (eds) *Consciousness and the Self: New Essays*, 76–100. Cambridge: Cambridge University Press.

Perry, J. (2012b) *Reference and Reflexivity*, 2nd edition. Stanford: CSLI.

Pinillos, A. (2011) Coreference and Meaning. *Philosophical Studies* 154: 301–24.

Pinillos, A. (2015) Millianism, Relationism, and Attitude Ascriptions. In A. Bianchi (ed.) *On Reference*, 322–34. Oxford: Oxford University Press.

Prior, A. (1957) *Time and Modality*. Oxford: Clarendon Press.

Prior, A. (1959) Thank Goodness That's Over. *Philosophy* 34: 12–17.

Prior, A. (1967) *Past, Present and Future*. Oxford: Clarendon Press.

Prosser, S. (2005) Cognitive Dynamics and Indexicals. *Mind & Language* 20: 369–91.

Prosser, S. (forthcoming). Shared Modes of Presentation. *Mind and Language*.

Putnam, H. (1975) The Meaning of 'Meaning'. In his *Mind, Language and Reality: Philosophical Papers*, vol. 2, 215–71. Cambridge: Cambridge University Press.

Recanati, F. (1987) Contextual Dependence and Definite Descriptions. *Proceedings of the Aristotelian Society* 87: 57–73.

Recanati, F. (1988) Rigidity and Direct Reference. *Philosophical Studies* 53: 103–17.

Recanati, F. (1990) Direct Reference, Meaning, and Thought. *Noûs* 24: 697–722.

Recanati, F. (1993) *Direct Reference: From Language to Thought*. Oxford: Blackwell.

Recanati, F. (1995) The Communication of First-Person Thoughts. In J. Biro and P. Kotatko (eds) *Frege: Sense and Reference One Hundred Years Later*, 95–102. Dordrecht: Kluwer.

Recanati, F. (1996) Domains of Discourse. *Linguistics and Philosophy* 19: 445–75.

Recanati, F. (1997a) The Dynamics of Situations. *European Review of Philosophy* 2: 41–75.

Recanati, F. (1997b) Can We Believe What We Do Not Understand? *Mind and Language* 12: 84–100.

Recanati, F. (2000) *Oratio Obliqua, Oratio Recta*. Cambridge, MA: MIT Press/Bradford Books.

Recanati, F. (2001) Modes of Presentation: Perceptual vs Deferential. In R. Stuhlmann-Laeisz, U. Nortmann and A. Newen (eds), *Building on Frege: New Essays on Sense, Content, and Concept*, 197–208. Stanford: CSLI Publications.

Recanati, F. (2002) Does Communication Rest on Inference ? *Mind and Language* 17: 105–26.

Recanati, F. (2007) *Perspectival Thought*. Oxford: Clarendon Press.

Recanati, F. (2010) *Truth-Conditional Pragmatics*. Oxford: Oxford University Press.

Recanati, F. (2012) *Mental Files*. Oxford: Oxford University Press.

Recanati, F. (2013a) Perceptual Concepts: In Defence of the Indexical Model. *Synthese* 190: 1841–55.

Recanati, F. (2013b) Mental Files: Replies to My Critics. In F. Salis (ed.) *Book Symposium on François Recanati's Mental Files*, 207–42. *Disputatio* 5/36.

Recanati, F. (2016) Indexical Thought: The Communication Problem. In M. Garcia-Carpintero and S. Torre (eds) *About Oneself*, 141–78. Oxford: Oxford University Press.

Recanati, F. (2017) Cognitive Dynamics. In M. de Ponte and K. Korta (eds) *Reference and Representation in Thought and Language*, 179–94. Oxford: Oxford University Press.

Recanati, F. (2018) Contextualism and Singular Reference. In J. Collins and T. Dobler (eds) *The Philosophy of Charles Travis: Language, Thought, and Perception*, 181–96. Oxford: Oxford University Press.

Recanati, F. (forthcoming) Coreference *De Jure*. In R. Goodman, J. Genone, and N. Kroll (eds) *Singular Thought and Mental Files*. Oxford: Oxford University Press.

Reddy, M. (1979) The Conduit Metaphor. In A. Ortony (ed.) *Metaphor and Thought*, 284–324. Cambridge: Cambridge University Press.

Reid, T. (1970) *An Inquiry into the Human Mind*. Chicago: University of Chicago Press.

Reinhart, T. (1983) *Anaphora and Semantic Interpretation*. London: Croom Helm.

Reinhart, T. (2006) *Interface Strategies*. Cambridge MA: MIT Press.

Reuland, E. (2011) *Anaphora and Language Design*. Cambridge, MA: MIT Press.

Roberts, C., Simons, M., Beaver, D., and Tonhauser, J. (2009) Presupposition, Conventional Implicature, and Beyond: A Unified Account of Projection. In *Proceedings of the Workshop on Presupposition*, ESSLLI '09, Bordeaux, July, 2009. Available at <http://www.ling.ohio-state.edu/~croberts/papers-roberts.html> accessed July 2016.

Roelofsen, F. (2010) Condition B Effects in Two Simple Steps. *Natural Language Semantics* 18: 115–40.

Safir, K. (1998) Abandoning Coreference. In Bermudez, J.L. (ed.) *Thought, Reference, and Experience*, 124–63. Oxford: Oxford University Press.

Safir, K. (2004) *The Syntax of Anaphora*. Oxford: Oxford University Press.

Salmon, N. (1986) Reflexivity. *Notre Dame Journal of Formal Logic* 27: 401–29.

Salmon, N. (1992) Reflections on Reflexivity. *Linguistics and Philosophy* 15: 53–63.

Schiffer, S. (1978) The Basis of Reference. *Erkenntnis* 13: 171–206.

Schlenker, P. (2005) Non-Redundancy: Towards a Semantic Reinterpretation of Binding Theory. *Natural Language Semantics* 13: 1–92.

Schroeter, L. (2007) The Illusion of Transparency. *Australasian Journal of Philosophy* 85: 597–618.

Schroeter, L. (2012) Bootstrapping Our Way to Samesaying. *Synthese* 189: 177–97.

Shoemaker, S. (1970) Persons and Their Pasts. *American Philosophical Quarterly* 7: 269–85.

Sider, T. (1996) All the World's a Stage. *Australasian Journal of Philosophy* 74: 433–53.

Sider, T. (2001) *Four-Dimensionalism*. Oxford: Clarendon Press.

Soames, S. (1994) Attitudes and Anaphora. *Philosophical Perspectives* 8: 251–72.

Soames, S. (2009) *Philosophical Essays, vol. II: The Philosophical Significance of Language*. Princeton: Princeton University Press.

Soames, S. (2010) Coordination Problems. *Philosophy and Phenomenological Research* 81: 464–74.

Soames, S. (2014) *Analytic Philosophy in America*. Princeton: Princeton University Press.

Sommers, F. (1982) *The Logic of Natural Language*. Oxford: Clarendon Press.

Spencer, C. (2006) Keeping Track of Objects in Conversation. In M. Garcia-Carpintero and J. Macia (eds) *Two-Dimensional Semantics*, 258–71. Oxford: Clarendon Press.

Sperber, D. (1994) Understanding Verbal Understanding. In J. Khalfa (ed.) *What is Intelligence*, 179–98. Cambridge: Cambridge University Press.

Sperber, D. (2000) Metarepresentation in an Evolutionary Perspective. In D. Sperber (ed.) *Metarepresentations*, 117–37. Oxford: Oxford University Press.

Sperber, D. and Wilson, D. (2002) Pragmatics, Modularity and Mind-reading. *Mind and Language* 17: 3–23.

Stalnaker, R. (1978) Assertion. *Syntax and Semantics* 9: 315–32.

Stalnaker, R. (1981) Indexical belief. *Synthese* 49: 129–51.

Stalnaker, R. (2003) *Ways a World Might Be*. Oxford: Clarendon Press.

Stalnaker, R. (2006) Responses. In J. Thomson and A. Byrne (eds) *Content and Modality: Themes from the Philosophy of Robert Stalnaker*, 250–95. Oxford: Clarendon Press.

Stalnaker, R. (2008) *Our Knowledge of the Internal World*. Oxford: Clarendon Press.

Stalnaker, R. (2014) *Context*. Oxford: Oxford University Press.

Strawson, P. (1971) *Logico-Linguistic Papers*. London: Methuen.

Strawson, P. (1974) *Subject and Predicate in Logic and Grammar*. London: Methuen.

Tayebi, S. (2012) Recanati on Communication of First-Person Thoughts. *Thought* 1: 210–18.

Taylor, K. (2003) *Reference and the Rational Mind*. Stanford: CSLI.

Textor, M. (2015) Frege's Theory of Hybrid Proper Names Extended. *Mind* 124: 823–47.

Torre, S. (2010) Centred Assertion. *Philosophical Studies* 150: 97–114.

Weber, C. (2013) Centred Communication. *Philosophical Studies* 166: S205–23.

Index*

---

* Neither the acknowledgments (pp. 17–18) nor the bibliographical references (pp. 161–71) have been indexed.

Printed and bound by CPI Group (UK) Ltd, Croydon, CR0 4YY